Contents

Series Editor's Preface

This series examines changing perspectives on a variety of educational issues and practices. It seeks to make accessible to the teacher and administrator, as well as to students, the most recent thinking, research, and development work in those areas. In education, ideas are presented all too often in a one-sided fashion, using rhetoric to disguise the lack of serious thought or supportive evidence. This series seeks to provoke balanced discussion on current issues based on a careful analysis of the most recent relevant information and research evidence.

The intention is to place current issues critically in an historical context but only so as to emphasise the changes which have subsequently taken place and the choices which currently face us. Recent thinking is described in as non-technical a way as the topic allows, with the emphasis on presenting complex ideas thoroughly but palatably. Practical examples are used to illustrate the theoretical ideas being presented, and so make the classroom and curricular applications more immediately apparent. Recognising the limited time teachers and administrators have, the series tries to cover each topic in a concise manner, indicating additional reading and references to more detailed information wherever appropriate.

In this book, Ian Selmes describes changing perspectives on the teaching of study skills. It is an issue of considerable interest at the moment. Schools are increasingly realising that pupils need systematic instruction in study skills. In the past, study skills were taught incidentally by subject teachers. Where a separate study skills course was provided, the emphasis was on distinct skills, such as note-taking or examination technique. And these traditional study skills courses seemed to have little influence on the ways pupils studied subsequently.

Ian Selmes, who is a practising teacher, investigated how pupils tackle their studying and what teachers expect them to do. This evidence was then used to suggest a more coherent approach to the teaching of study skills. Pupils need to recognise the active part they play in extracting meaning and in developing effective strategies

STUDY SKILLS

Ian Selmes

HODDER AND STOUGHTON
LONDON   SYDNEY   AUCKLAND   TORONTO

Changing Perspectives in Education

Series Editor: Noel Entwistle, BSc, PhD

The Core Curriculum   Gordon Kirk
Improving Study Skills   Ian Selmes
Understanding Classroom Learning   Noel Entwistle
Research on Education   John Nisbet
Appraising Teacher Quality   John Wilson

British Library Cataloguing in Publication Data
Selmes, Ian
    Improving study skills.—(Changing
    perspectives in education)
    1. Study, Method of
    I. Title   II. Series
    371.3′028′12   LB1049

    ISBN 0-340-39700-4

First published 1987
Copyright © 1987 I. P. Selmes
Second impression 1988

*Photoset by
Rowland Phototypesetting Ltd,
Bury St Edmunds, Suffolk.
Printed in Great Britain
for Hodder and Stoughton Educational,
a division of Hodder and Stoughton Ltd,
Mill Road, Dunton Green, Sevenoaks, Kent by
Richard Clay Ltd, Bungay*

geared to differing purposes. Using a framework derived from the research findings, Ian Selmes suggests the sort of activities which will help pupils to become more effective learners.

Noel Entwistle
University of Edinburgh
1986

The Author

Ian Selmes is a geography teacher at Merchiston Castle School, Edinburgh. He has recently completed a part-time PhD degree which involved developing and evaluating a study skills programme within his school. He has also organised regular seminars for Edinburgh teachers to discuss the teaching of study skills, and has been actively involved in the curriculum changes currently being introduced in geography both for GCSE and Scottish Standard grade examinations.

Author's Preface

There are other books about the processes of studying. However, most of these books set out to instil a single method of studying which is supported neither by classroom teachers' experience nor research evidence of pupils' learning. Moreover, in consulting a selection of these 'cookbooks' their idiosyncratic and contradictory nature becomes apparent. Other books with a less prescriptive approach are either written with higher education students in mind, or fail to relate their advice to the type of tasks which secondary school pupils experience. None provides a sound basis for the teaching of study skills in schools.

This book describes research and development in teaching study skills and what constitutes good practice in such assistance. Throughout the book I shall be referring to the research project which formed the basis of my PhD thesis entitled 'Approaches to Learning at Secondary School; their Identification and Facilitation'. This sought an understanding of how pupils go about their studying and of the demands of the tasks they are required to undertake at different stages in secondary education. The nature of appropriate study skills assistance was established and materials were developed, piloted and evaluated. This book includes a description of these research findings, and invites teachers to consider how to enhance their pupils' learning skill by adaptation of the ideas, materials and methods of evaluation discussed.

It is argued that secondary school teachers should be concerned with the process of learning and not just the content. In the appropriate teaching of study skills there is a key to more effective learning and teaching.

Ian P. Selmes
1986

Acknowledgments

I should like to thank the pupils and staff of the various Edinburgh schools that participated in the study which forms the basis of this book; Alistair Hector, Robert Russell and numerous other colleagues at Merchiston Castle School and in Edinburgh's Teaching of Study Skills Group, for their interest, involvement and stimulation over the years; Noel Entwistle for his encouragement in research and preparation of this book; and Louise Hardy for patiently preparing the manuscript.

Ian P. Selmes

PART ONE
Why Teach Study Skills?

1

Conventional Study Skills Assistance

Teachers in secondary schools are trained to teach a subject. We are subject enthusiasts. Our role is to communicate knowledge and skills inherent in our subject. Through experience, we become aware of particular difficulties some pupils have in studying our subject, and our curriculum development often focuses on means of alleviating these difficulties by changes in subject content. At times we also discuss difficulties in terms of problem solving, though usually in a specific way. But do we pay enough attention to the more general difficulties which pupils may experience in learning?

In 1981 a group of experienced teachers and researchers were brought together, by the British Library Research and Development Department and the Schools Council, to consider the promotion of study skills. Their conclusion was that 'schools, which are concerned with learning above all else, find great difficulty in teaching pupils how to learn'.[1] Indeed, surveys of study difficulties experienced by pupils in British schools have identified a range of common study difficulties so extensive that they cover virtually all learning tasks pupils undertake (Table 1.1). Pupils performing these tasks, and their teachers, described general difficulties of inertia, concentration, dependency on the teacher, and motivation, and of how to undertake the tasks. The significance of these findings is enhanced with each difficulty having been described by over 30%[2] or 50%[3,4] of the pupils in independent surveys. The evidence is unequivocal. Most pupils do, in fact, report difficulties with the process of studying.

The consequences of pupils commonly experiencing fundamental difficulties with their studying spread beyond schools. The proportion of pupils leaving school without paper qualifications has

Table 1.1   Pupils' difficulties in studying

Difficulties in studying	Expressed by pupils	Expressed by pupils' teachers
Making independent notes in class from teachers' talk and from books	*	*
Finding relevant information in books	*	
Organising background reading	*	*
Recalling what has been read	*	*
Assessing arguments in print	*	*
Planning written work	*	*
Relating evidence to arguments	*	*
Being critical of one's writing		*
Concentrating on facts and descriptions		*
Remembering information or ideas	*	
Organising revision	*	
Reliance on rote learning		*
Organising study time and effort	*	
Balancing time devoted to subjects	*	
Meeting deadlines	*	
Overcoming inertia	*	
Adjusting to greater independence	*	*
Lack of independent initiative		*
Dependence on teachers		*

(This table is an amalgam of the research findings in references 2–7.)

troubled everyone concerned with education. Despite marked improvement in recent years, in 1983–84 9.5% of English school-leavers[8] and 26.2% of those in Scotland[9] failed to be graded in any public examination. Criticism of pupils' learning has also come from tertiary educators and from potential employers. Teaching methods in schools have been criticised for developing rigid habits in pupils' learning methods and a dependence on routines and on teachers. Such an outcome is in direct conflict with the aim of independence which is fundamental to most syllabuses. The effect of external examinations on teaching methods and learning approaches in Britain may well have interfered with the development of pupils' understanding.[10] Knowledge may be acquired from the study of particular subjects but industrialists complain that their recruits are not equipped to use knowledge in ways which are relevant to the world outside the classroom. As a result of their school experiences, students and employees are seen to exhibit a lack of competence in learning.

It becomes apparent that pupils, employers and tertiary educators might be justified in thinking that teachers have been too concerned with *what* is taught and learnt, and not concerned enough with *how* pupils learn. But it would be too easy to caricature schools as treating pupils like young sportsmen with potential, surrounding them with good players who merely encourage them to play well without giving any systematic coaching on skills. Major projects by both the National Foundation for Educational Research (NFER)[2] and the Scottish Council for Research in Education (SCRE)[11] have found that teachers are concerned about the methods of pupils' learning. As teachers, our difficulty is often in understanding how to help. In this book the processes of pupils' learning and the question of how to improve their skills of studying are both explored. But first it is important to examine what is already being done in schools to teach study skills.

The tradition of study skills teaching

Recent surveys have sought to establish the extent and nature of study skills teaching in British secondary schools. The Teaching of Study Skills Project,[2] based at the National Foundation for Educational Research (NFER), investigated provision for 16–19 year olds in England and Wales. Approaches to all the local education authorities found many schools and colleges about to develop courses and keen to receive advice. As many as 76 institutions had already undertaken some development. In 47 of these, special courses were organised either as induction courses or early in sixth-form or further education curricula. Another 6 offered study skills as a general studies option and 18 laid the responsibility on form teachers. In Scotland, a questionnaire survey of all secondary schools[12] led to almost 30% of the schools providing outlines of their current practice in teaching study skills. Short courses or discussion groups were often included within social education classes or were taught by guidance teachers. A fifth of these schools indicated that the topic was left for the subject teachers to deal with.

As in England and Wales, most provision was directed at pupils taking public examinations at the upper end of secondary school, and assistance in study skills was often seen as a preparation for examinations rather than as an aid to improving learning as a whole.

Despite this apparently encouraging level of study skills provision, evaluation of the study skills courses has shown that their effectiveness has been limited. It appears that headteachers may have been over-optimistic in their belief that subject teachers deal with study skills effectively. The NFER project investigated the impact of 24 of the courses by interview and questionnaire. Most of the teachers involved were content just to raise their pupils' awareness of study methods. Yet barely half the pupils interviewed thought that they had had effective help with their studying difficulties. Some pupils were very positive about the advice, offering comments such as:

> I feel that the college has made a great effort in teaching study skills in relation to the subjects you are doing. This has been a great help and without it I would be at a total loss.

Yet very few pupils considered they had been assisted to overcome general problems such as inertia. When advice was recalled it tended to be in the form of tips rather than a more fundamental awareness of the process of learning. Pupils said that they had rejected general tips because they might interfere with their existing methods. The NFER project also criticised the organisation of the general study skills courses. The courses evaluated hardly met even the limited objective of their developers. Since they were rarely planned in collaboration with subject teachers not involved with the general course, these teachers questioned the relevance of the advice given to subject lessons and the curriculum. Moreover, few pupils described follow-up sessions in normal lessons. So there seem to have been few opportunities to apply skills in practice.

Why was this the case? What was the content of these courses and how were they taught?

In secondary schools the traditional assumption has been that pupils learn the skills of studying through the work they are required to do in their different subjects. The teaching of study skills has rarely been a specified curriculum aim.[1] Where there have been policies for teaching study skills, such as those described in the two surveys above,[2,12] the responsibility for organising advice has often been given to subject or form teachers. The NFER Teaching of Study Skills Project[2] came to the conclusion that the most effective approach would be to develop better study skills through everyday subject teaching. And the SCRE's project on Writing Across the Curriculum in secondary schools[11] found teachers to be very willing to contribute to the development of writing skills. However the SCRE project, and a series of research studies carried out by Roberts,[7] Ruddock,[13] Selmes,[6] and Thompson,[4] have all identified a gap between the aims and the practices of teachers in promoting pupils' study skills. Many teachers seem to assume that the necessary skills would have been taught by someone else or would develop independently by maturation.[14] It has also been suggested that the extent of study skills teaching has been limited by overloaded subject syllabuses[6] and uncertainty about how to teach the necessary skills.[4,15]

With such findings it is perhaps not surprising that many pupils have been unaware of having obtained useful study skills assistance from their teachers. Moreover, on the occasions where teachers have made study skills provisions, they have, necessarily, been dependent on the published advice readily available.

Teachers wanting to assist pupils with their study skills have not been starved of published advice. A burgeoning library of books has grown up. But what advice is given and how effective is it likely to be?

The NFER project in England and Wales and the Scottish survey found that virtually all the courses reported were based on specific books. Of these books, the most popular were Tony Buzan's *Use Your Head*[16] and Derek Rowntree's *Learn How to Study*.[17] These two books were also commonly recommended to pupils. Both are intended to be self-contained courses, offering the key to success. Buzan's claim was that:

> By the time you have finished this book you should be able to study more effectively, solve problems more readily, read faster and more efficiently, and . . . you will be able to develop your own ways of thinking.

The advice in these books tends to suggest that by doing certain 'simple'things learning problems will disappear. For instance, in terms of reading the essence of Buzan's advice is:

Instead of insisting that they remove their fingers [from the page] we should ask them to move their fingers faster . . . practice taking in more than one line at a time . . . Turning pages as fast as possible, attempting to see as many words per page as possible . . . If a decision is made to do better, then poor performance will automatically improve.

The advice also tends to be generalised, and also rather inflexible as it is applied only to a standard situation. Rowntree's advice is followed by frequent questions to which there is only one 'correct' answer. For example, with regard to reading, the learner is asked to complete these statements before progressing:

1 Read the (*title*) page.
2 Read the author's remarks, or (*preface*).
3 Read the table of (*contents*).
4 Leaf quickly through the entire (*book*).
5 How long do you think you might need to spend on this overall survey? Between (*5*) and (*30*) minutes.

In these most popular books and other sources of advice, many of the techniques suggested are quite complicated and yet they have not proved to be any more effective then the methods commonly used in schools. For example, a commonly recommended technique for reading is the mnemonic SQ3R (survey, question, read, recite, recall).[18] This, and other such advice, is essentially unrealistic by demanding much more time than pupils have available. For instance, one strategy for remembering indicates that:

By careful review of your learning, you will retain much of the information that you would otherwise forget within a day. Your reviewing of information should be programmed like this:
(a) A few minutes after the lesson or period of study, quickly go over the information.
(b) Twenty-four hours later, review again.
(c) At the end of the week, review what has been covered in that week.
(d) At the end of the month, review that month's learning.
(e) After six months, review again.[19]

Applying this advice to one topic would certainly be effective, but pupils' reactions to this as general advice can be imagined.

There is another major problem. The advice suggested in different books is conflicting.[20] For example, one book[21] claims that it is better to have a clear head than a few extra facts read the night before an examination. Another book[22] advises that even if no work is done at any other time, a lot should be done just before an exam. Such contradictions are to be expected with each author proposing study methods that they, as individuals, have found useful. The advice is not based on any underlying rationale devised from a systematic investigation of pupils' learning processes.

The sources of published advice which have been found to form the basis of most study skills assistance in schools clearly do not provide a sound basis for such teaching. Their self-contained, prescriptive content is superficially attractive as it provides what seem to be well defined 'facts'. However, in emphasising single 'best' methods these 'cookbooks'[23] are directed at the general category of 'student' through the attributes of a stereotyped 'ideal' student – and a higher education student at that. These models of organised efficiency serve to emphasise the difference between the individual pupil and this 'ideal'. In consequence the advice would be alienating to many pupils who already feel somewhat inadequate. There is also a gap between 'knowing' and 'doing'. Without opportunities to practice even useful advice, pupils are unlikely to put it into practice. Furthermore, even when applied, the inflexibility of the advice is likely to foster both dependence on the teacher and rigid study habits. It is hardly surprising that pupils experiencing such advice have not found it all that helpful.

How then might study skills be taught more appropriately in schools? There have already been a variety of attempts to provide more effective study skills teaching – although few of them have any clear rationale.

Alternative approaches to study skills teaching

In traditional study skills teaching the content has depended on an individual's 'expert' opinion of what is required, and has involved prescription of how a task should be performed. Yet when learners have been asked to describe their normal study methods,[24] a variety of approaches to learning have been mentioned. A common feature of these varying approaches is that successful learners are well organised. In contrast, low achievers are found not to know or realise how to organise their studying. They also tend to transfer the blame for their poor performance away from themselves and on to peers, teachers or the institution. Responses to questionnaires based on these interview responses suggest that successful learners tend to think about what they learn in ways which extend their previous understanding. And they confirm that this search for understanding is supported by systematically identifying and using skills appropriate to the demands of a specific task.

How then might such skill in studying be acquired? Unless pupils have been encouraged to monitor the requirements of a task and to have gained a working knowledge of actions and their outcomes in relation to various task requirements, demands for long-term recall and independent studying are likely to be fruitless. Two characteristics of assistance seem necessary for learner-control to be fostered over how study tasks are undertaken. If the pupil is provided with a framework in which to structure his or her thoughts and actions about study tasks, then a basis for an ability to plan ahead may be laid. Practice in the use of different strategies, together with discussion of these experiences with peers and teachers, could then help study skills to develop.

A framework for considering the learning process has been suggested by the Centre for the Study of Human Learning at Brunel University.[25] This is one of the few examples of study skills underpinned by a clear rationale. In the process of reading the sequence of ideas involves purpose, strategy, outcome and review, the process being cyclical:

> When you approach a reading task you clarify your purpose, choose an appropriate strategy, specify and assess the outcome of your reading, and then check back to see that your purpose is accomplished.

The sequence of ideas provides a structure for the process of reading and identifies points within the process where assistance might be provided to develop reading ability. This framework could also provide a language for considering the learning process with regard to any study task.

Other techniques involve presenting the study skills training in an entirely different way. One approach, promoted by Alex Main,[26] is to base it on individualised, non-directive counselling. By investigating perceptions of difficulties, exploring them through discussion and then seeking alternative methods, students are encouraged to make their own decisions about how to undertake studying. Such raising of awareness and active participation in studying helps to bridge the gap between 'knowing' and 'doing'. Yet schools could not offer such individualised counselling on a widespread basis, although it might be used to cope with extreme cases of difficulty.

Another technique, which encourages self-awareness in studying through group discussions, has been advocated by Graham Gibbs.[27] His approach recognises the need for learners to examine for themselves the content and processes of learning. In groups of between twelve and forty people a common task is given to provide a focus for subsequent discussion. The way the task has been tackled is then discussed in pairs, in fours and finally with the whole group. The aims are to focus on the purpose of the task and to identify the range of successful techniques adopted by different students.

How effective might this alternative approach to study skills teaching be in schools? Gibbs' approach does require confidence in discussion and relies entirely on the learners' own experiences of studying. Providing the exercises involve tasks pupils actually meet in schools, they will probably have something to contribute to the pool of ideas. Some teachers may feel that a non-directive approach would give too much attention to ineffective procedures and may be a time-consuming and cumbersome means of drawing attention to more effective ways of studying. Indeed, pupils may welcome the teachers' experiences within the discussion, providing they are not presented as being the one 'right' way to study. The National Foundation for Educational Research's project[2] reported a trial of Gibbs' materials with school pupils, its impact being evaluated by teachers' questionnaire. The teachers indicated that they were happy using the materials, finding the structured group discussions useful. The pupils were thought to have benefited from the experience. Even so, the materials were considered to be difficult to adapt to the specific demands of subjects. Pupils did not find it easy to be self-analytical and teachers found it difficult to be non-directive. It could have been that, at school, the 16–19 year old pupils in the trial did not experience the task demands assumed to be necessary by Gibbs. Though teachers of study skills would be justified in thinking such an approach was more likely to help develop pupils' study skills than the traditional approach, a fundamental weakness remains in not knowing the nature of the tasks pupils do perform at school.

For aspiring teachers of study skills there are already a number of other publications which adopt an active approach and recognise that secondary school pupils' experiences can provide a starting point for enhancing their study skill. These include the books by Hamblin,[28] Irving[29] and Marland.[1] However, none of these alternative approaches to study skills teaching has been based on a convincing theoretical rationale or an analysis of pupils' actual study activities. These are weaknesses which this book seeks to overcome, by presenting a new perspective on improving study skills. It uses research into how pupils carry out classroom tasks to develop a rationale for study skills activities in schools.

The findings from the research[6,30] are presented in Part Two. The main aim of this research was to develop a better understanding of the studying carried out by secondary school pupils. The ultimate goal was to devise an effective study skills course for use in schools, and a means of assessing its effects on pupils' practices. Interviews were carried out to discover how pupils actually undertook study tasks, and why they adopted different approaches within the normal school curriculum. Both pupils and teachers were interviewed to establish the nature of the task demands pupils experienced. Pupils were found to vary their approach to a task according to a teacher's classroom practices. However, the demands of study tasks at any one level in secondary schools tended to required a consistent approach, the demands only varying between age groups.

The final part of the book invites teachers to consider what might be done within a school to improve pupils' skill in studying. The nature of appropriate study skills assistance is considered and a course, developed out of the research findings, is described in detail. Evaluation of the course and any study skills provision is then considered, as is the effect of improving pupils' study skills on teaching and learning in secondary schools. Teachers should be able to adapt the ideas and materials contained in this book to their own requirements.

PART TWO
What does Studying Involve?

2

Contrasting Approaches to Studying

The aim of learning is to acquire knowledge and understanding. These are developed through the processes of teaching and studying. When the learner's mind was likened to a vessel waiting to be loaded with information, it was considered appropriate to express the results of learning in terms of *how much* had been learnt. Didactic teaching of a whole class often led to a factual test with a mark out of ten; a measure of how much knowledge had been recalled before progressing to the next body of information. Educators now realise that learning is not such a simple process of acquiring pieces of factual knowledge. We recognise that pupils each have their own personalities, motivations, experiences and perceptions, which will influence their learning. Moreover, the capacity to learn is no longer considered as entirely an innate ability; neither is it one in which an individual will be equally adept in all situations. Teachers and pupils have ample firsthand experience that learning is an inefficient exercise fraught with difficulties and for which useful guidance is rare. For the effectiveness of learning to be improved, attention must be focused at least as much upon the process of learning as on what is to be learned. This means an unfamiliar question has to be answered: how do pupils actually undertake study tasks?

Of course we all know how we, personally, go about particular tasks. But, as was argued in the previous chapter, there is no single 'best' way of undertaking all study tasks for any individual or even of a single task for all individuals. What is needed is an understanding of the range of approaches pupils adopt towards the study tasks they experience in schoolwork. The problem for teachers is in looking at learning from the pupils' point of view. As subject experts and enthusiasts, teachers' concern has been more with how the material might be taught than with what makes the material difficult. For the relatively successful learners who join Britain's all-graduate teaching profession, it is very difficult to appreciate the variety of the inappropriate strategies of learning which pupils adopt. Through pupils' collective descriptions of how they learn we can start to gain a better understanding of their normal learning process.

For this understanding to be communicated and applied in schools, a language is required for describing how pupils learn. Such a language might be adapted from one already used in higher education. The learning behaviour of students has received a lot of attention in recent years, and a distinction between 'deep' and 'surface' approaches to learning has been made.[31,32] The two categories of approach contrast the learner's intention in, and their process of, learning. A deep approach involves the learner in seeking a personal understanding of the meaning or what was inferred in a discourse. A surface approach involves the reproduction of facts or ideas, fulfilling the requirements of a task unreflectively. These general descriptions are widely applicable categories. They have been identified in a variety of disciplines and countries and are more fully discussed in *Understanding Classroom Learning*, in this series. Academically successful students have been found to adopt different approaches to tasks according to the individual's perception of the situation, or context, experienced. How do secondary school pupils describe their approaches to common study tasks?

Approaches to studying

The descriptions of approach to be found below derive from an investigation of thirteen pupils studying A levels or Scottish Higher grades.[6,30] Between them the pupils made forty-six descriptions of approaches to tasks across the curriculum – in English, French, German, Economics, History, Geography, Mathematics, Physics, Chemistry and Biology. Similarities in their descriptions represent a body of first-hand experiences of pupils' behaviour in studying such syllabuses.[6] The approaches described throw light on how pupils go about their studying, in a manner whose relevance and immediacy to the classroom is clear to see.

The research which forms the basis of this book[6,30] sought to develop a sound empirical understanding of the nature of common study tasks, how pupils undertake such tasks, and the factors which influence their approach to the tasks. From these findings a pilot version of Chapter 5's Learning to Learn course was developed to foster pupils' control over their learning methods. It was evaluated with the techniques described in Chapter 6 and modified accordingly.

Pupils' descriptions of a deep approach towards a task fell into three main categories: attempting personal integration of the material; seeking relationships between materials; and extracting meaning from the material involved. Each of these categories have opposing characteristics which were the pupils' descriptions of a surface approach: passivity in carrying out a task; isolating aspects of the material or task; and memorisation of the material. The defining characteristics of each of these categories of approach are shown in Tables 2.1 and 2.2

Though teachers may not be familiar with looking at learning from the pupils' perspective, these contrasts in approach that pupils adopt are readily recognisable in the defining characteristics and in illustrations from the interviews.

A deep approach is indicated when a pupil attempts to create a personal interpretation of the material. (All quotes which follow are taken from the research undertaken in 1985 and 1986.)[6,30]

Interviewer: Where you're writing these out, are you trying to produce an argument backed up by evidence or what sort of structure do you have?

Pupil: In Biology nothing is ever clear cut so you've got to represent two, three or perhaps even four arguments and then try and say at the end which one seems most likely but why it might not be likely . . . if you see what I mean.

The contrasting passivity of a surface approach would be seen when a pupil depends on external influences (such as the teacher) to define the task, or does not think about carrying out the task:

Interviewer: And these notes, are they ones that you make?

Table 2.1 Deep approach categories and their defining characteristics

---

D1   *Personal Integration*

Intention to create personal interpretation of material.
Emphasises importance of comparing personal interpretation with that of someone else.
Indicates desire to relate task to own personal situation outside the immediate context.
Intention to link personal ideas/experiences to subject matter of task.
Indicates desire to relate task/concept to real life situations.
Sees task as part of personal development.

D2   *Interrelationships*

Intention to relate parts of task to each other.
Intention to relate task to other relevant knowledge.
Relating what is known about another problem to a new problem.
Relating previously studied materials to new materials or new materials with future materials.
Intention to relate materials from different sources.
Actively thinks about relations between parts of the material.
Attempts to relate aspects of a problem.

D3   *Meaningfulness*

Intention to focus on the meaning of the content.
Intention to think about the underlying structure of task.
Attempts to use part of material to represent whole or a text to represent a type of text.

Pupil: No. In general we get given duplicated notes and have to copy them out.

Interviewer: Word for word?

Pupil: Or adding in bits if you want. In Chemistry I haven't actually done any extra notemaking.

When a pupil connects the various parts of a task then a deep approach can also be recognised. This might involve linking past experiences with the present task or, perhaps, relating materials from different sources.

Table 2.2   Surface approach categories and their defining
characteristics

S1   *Isolating*

Focusing on procedural elements in task.
Tendency to treat material as isolated from other materials.
Task seen to comprise discrete parts.
Focus on elements of task.

S2   *Memorisation*

Task context perceived to require recall of material.
Task defined as a memory task by the pupil.
Pupil indicates intention to memorise the material.

S3   *Passivity*

Task defined by someone else.
Indicating unreflective or passive approach to task.
Indicating dependence on the teacher.
Treating the material externally.

Interviewer: And you said that these [notes] were made in lessons as you go along. What do you actually mean by that?

Pupil: Well, um . . . Teacher will put certain things up on the board like diagrams, graphs, equations, and how to derive these equations, but will talk you through a subject. What I do is um, take down what is on the board and make extra notes on what comes up in class and then after class I will go and get the textbook out as well and rewrite the notes, adding bits in from the textbook.

However, if a pupil isolates rather than integrates aspects of the material or task, then a surface approach has been adopted. Such an occasion could involve a task being seen to comprise discrete parts:

Interviewer: And are you asked to write . . . is it an essay in the English sense of an essay, a piece of writing of that long length?

> *Pupil*:   Well I find with that sort of [Chemistry] essay where you're given certain things to write about, it doesn't really connect very well; it's not sort of as fluent as you write in an English essay. It's more facts.

Another manifestation of a deep approach would be when a pupil intends or acts to extract meaning from the material:

> *Interviewer*: Are you looking for characterisation, what individual characters do, or are you looking for events?
>
> *Pupil*:   I think the idea is to single out a character for analysis and also different themes of the book; tell what it's doing. If it's got any other meaning than . . . the basic story. If it's trying to get a message across.

Alternatively, a concentration upon memorisation of the material would suggest a surface approach, whether by intention or by activity:

> *Interviewer*: For instance, if we take History and those dictated notes; what do you see as the purpose of those?
>
> *Pupil*:   They give the information that I have to learn for the syllabus for the History Higher, in fairly short sentences, so I can pick up the information that I need to learn for the exam fairly easily.

In such descriptions teachers and parents will begin to recognise the approaches to studying adopted by children that they have observed. The reality of the deep and surface approaches does provide a means of conceptualising the learning process. It can be seen to be relevant from both the teachers' and the pupils' perspective. How then might these approaches be identified within particular tasks?

Approaches within study tasks

Teachers structure their lessons and pupils experience their work in an interrelated series of study tasks. Of these tasks, reading, making notes, and writing answers to specific instructions are probably the most common. The contrasting characteristics of deep and surface approaches are readily apparent within these tasks.

Reading with a deep approach might be recognised when various materials are related to help achieve understanding, or when reading is viewed as a part of personal development:

Interviewer: How would you extract information from this diagram . . . what do you actually do to see what it tells you?

Pupil: Well, you look at the diagram and then see if it says anything about it in the following pages.

Interviewer: What has to be done [when reading]?

Pupil: You just can't read hundreds of books in a year. You've got to have read a fair amount of literature . . . your vocabulary will improve with reading. You can't just get it overnight.

A surface approach towards the task of reading could involve a concentration upon the facts or an intention to memorise the material:

Interviewer: What other things do you find involved in studying Chemistry?

Pupil: We'll be told to read the book out of class . . . then we go through it in class, normally just skim through it picking out the more important bits.

Interviewer: And what if you were in a limited amount of time?

Pupil: Well I'd just read it through very quickly.

Interviewer: With what purpose?

Pupil: To get to know as much about it as you can in a short time, to take in as much as you can in a short while.

Notes may be made from various stimuli, and a deep approach to this task might be seen when independent efforts are made to relate parts of the material or to apply material in a new context:

Interviewer: So you come to a consensus view of the whole class. Is it then that notes tend to be made, or afterwards?

Pupil: The teacher says, you read the book, do you not think the character was or shouldn't have been angry at so and so. You're trying to prove an argument. And so we give him arguments, but we can add what we think ourselves. If you take down his notes, he doesn't often include what we say.

Interviewer: When you are watching videos, what are you doing, what do you think the aim is?
Pupil: It's getting to . . . mainly broadening and complementing what you've already done. Perhaps giving more specific examples of something we've studied in class and notes are occasionally taken.

Notes which are not made independently and are not the product of the pupil's own thought are, however, a common manifestation of a surface approach:

Interviewer: Could you perhaps describe to me how these notes are actually made?
Pupil: Well, the teacher will actually write up on the board the calculations, [we] copy them down. And also we get given notes about how to do the calculations.
Interviewer: On a piece of paper?
Pupil: No. The teacher usually writes them up on the board or points them out and we take them down.

As a task, writing can take many forms, from brief answers to essays and projects. When performed with a deep approach, efforts might be apparent to develop an understanding by relating aspects, or to show that understanding by producing a personal interpretation:

Interviewer: And how do you come by this understanding, what sort of things do you do to develop it?
Pupil: Well really what you've got to do is work through everything until you're quite sure you can see exactly how everything was arrived at. You've got to look at how you get there. That's how you come to understand it.

Interviewer: Do you think there is any purpose in producing this personal interpretation?
Pupil: Well, yes. It gives you a chance to think for yourself

and it's always useful to set down your interpretation of a thing so you can compare your ideas with
an [expert's] idea. To see where you contrast and
where you compare.

In comparison, surface approaches towards writing may be recognised when the task is perceived to require recall of material or is
undertaken in a mechanistic way:

Interviewer: And what do you see as the purpose of these
exercises?
Pupil: Well, there's a lot of techniques to answering A
level questions and if you answer a lot of past
questions you pick up that technique.

Interviewer: And you've got this title. What do you then do to
decide what to write down and how to write it?
Pupil: Well, I think the best idea is to get the notes on your
ideas, then write it down, then check for tenses,
check for graves and anything missed out, correct it
all, then write it out again.

In these descriptions the practical differences are made clear
between deep and surface approaches to everyday study tasks
carried out by pupils. Yet being able to identify the symptoms
without being able to recognise the cause represents incomplete
learning about the process of learning; knowledge without understanding. What is it that causes a pupil to adopt a particular
approach towards a specific task? How consistent is a pupil's
approach towards studying?

Causes of approach adopted

On reading pupils' descriptions of how they have approached study
tasks, it is apparent that what they have done has not always been of
their own free will. A requirement to conform with a subject's or a
teacher's conventions can restrict and direct a pupil's approach.
This is after all the role of a teacher, to guide a pupil in his learning.
For this to be done effectively, aims and means must coincide. An
understanding of how specific influences precipitate one or other

approach is needed if appropriate and effective study skills advice is to be provided.

As well as describing how they undertook a task, the pupil interviewees often volunteered reasons for their adoption of a particular approach. These causes related to four situations, or contexts, in which a task was experienced: the methods of assessment; the formality of the teaching; dependence on the teacher; and the time available. Personal characteristics of motivation and anxiety were also shown to be influential within certain contexts.

The nature of assessment is probably the most influential factor. Both the methods used and the pupil's perception of the demands these make are important. A pupil's goals and feelings about the task itself, as well as about others – such as teachers, parents and peers – involved with the pupil, will affect this perception. Thus assessments which are 'closed'[1] (demanding the reproduction of facts or the memorisation of material), and which are extrinsically motivating (involving vocational or academic goals and reward or punishment beyond the task), are always linked to a surface approach. For instance:

> We always do a practical once a week because there are quite a lot of practicals for A level that have been done in the past and then are repeated. So what we are doing is we are working through every single practical A level that has ever been done. Which means that when it comes to the A level [exam] we have a chance of doing really well in one of those practicals.

Assessments which cause a deep approach to be adopted are very different. They might involve 'open' questions,[1] allowing a variety of responses and encouraging the use of a number of sources sought by the pupil. Opportunity might be provided for including personal views or experiences. Such assessments are intrinsically motivating. These contrasts in context and approach are obvious in this pupil's description of how he wrote about the advantages and disadvantages of holidaying abroad:

> . . . [I] decide what I'm actually going to write about. That's done by the frame of mind that I am in at the moment. First of all decide whether you are for or against and then say to yourself, why am I for it and write down a list, and why am I against it and write down a list, and write away.

On discovering that the first pupil was discussing practicals in Physics and the second pupil describing an essay in German, the reaction might be to see the difference as merely reflecting a contrast in subject matter. The nature of different disciplines creates differences in the way they are taught and assessed. Certainly some subjects possess a greater body of fact whilst others are more interpretative. But the means used to reach a desired outcome must do so effectively. No subject requires just the memorisation of facts. Yet, if the type of assessment employed only encourages surface approaches, then such a limited result will occur. Equally, interpretation without content is impossible. A balance of approaches fostered by a variety of assessments would help to develop the knowledge and understanding components of real learning.

This creation of different situations to bring about appropriate approaches for the development of a particular result is surely what teaching is all about. Without a practical language to consider the process of learning and a detailed and verifiable grasp of how the process is influenced, effective and creative teaching has had to be intuitive in the past. This need no longer be the case.

When a pupil experiences very formal teaching methods, such as dictation or direct instruction, then surface approaches can be expected to occur – with all the implications this has for the learning outcome. Similar effects can be expected when a pupil is caused to be dependent on the teacher through being provided with rigid structure or content, or by doing as the teacher does in order to please the teacher:

> Well normally we get given notes . . . we get handed out sheets and sheets of notes . . . which we will discuss in class, which we go off and copy out word for word, odd alterations but practically word for word because the wording he uses is the wording you really want to reproduce. It's better that way.

When the teaching is less formal, as in discussion, or where there is an unconcealed intention to promote understanding, a deep approach is facilitated. This approach will also be fostered when a pupil is able to feel more independent of the teacher:

> There's sometimes literature notes given on describing a poem or something. The teacher generally gives us notes on the poem and

we take our own notes . . . describing the poem, being able to understand it more clearly.

Situations in which time is felt to be restricted tend to produce anxiety in pupils and limit studying to a surface approach. Time is often very tight in assessment tasks, but in the classroom the teacher has direct control over the time available for carrying out tasks. In the absence of time being perceived by pupils as too restricted, they will be liberated to adopt a deep approach towards a task. Restrictive contexts will cause anxiety and an intention to memorise materials (a surface approach), whilst in less restrictive contexts a search for understanding (a deep approach) will take place even when attempting the same task. One pupil illustrated this most succinctly:

> I find in Physics, the practical exam itself, you end up having to do two experiments in a set time and they tell you to a certain extent how to do the experiment and you've just to get your results. Whereas in real Physics experiments, you know, as a scientist, you wouldn't have a time limit and you wouldn't know so much of what to do. So I don't know if it's a good test because some people get into a panic about timing. If you get held up in one experiment you can't do the other properly.

The panoply of causes linked by the pupil interviewees to the adoption of a particular approach towards a task are summarised in Table 2.3. Yet no pupil described exclusively deep or surface approaches to all tasks met across the subjects studied. Table 2.4 does show that a consistent approach to one or more tasks across the subjects studied was apparent for all but two of the interviewees. However, a consistent deep approach towards one task was matched by a consistent surface approach, or a variable approach, in other tasks performed by the same pupil. Variation in approach is not just found between pupils but also within a pupil's studying and even within a task, as this pupil explained:

Interviewer: Perhaps you could tell me about the range of these tasks in Geography?

Pupil: Well, first in class, we've got to make notes, which is different from a lot of other subjects because in a lot of other subjects notes are dictated to us. [In

Geography] usually you get the main title and then a question or say a title . . . all you've got to do is give a brief background to the place, give some information about it, then you listen for the advantages and disadvantages that are spoken during class and write them down.

Table 2.3 The nature of contextual and personal influences on senior pupils' approach to specific study tasks

	Perception of influence associated with:	
Influences	Surface approach	Deep approach
teaching methods	formal or repetitive	informal
studying tasks	closed	open
type of assessment	focus on facts or closed response	focus on meaning or open response
level of dependence	high	low
time available	insufficient or restricted	ample or unrestricted
motivation	extrinsic	intrinsic
anxiety	high	low

Differences in the context in which incidences of a task were experienced were therefore described as the cause of the variability in approach. If the nature of a task imposed upon a pupil was similar across various subjects, or if the pupil was independent of the imposed structure but had habitual practices, consistency was described. But, if the nature of a task met between subjects or if the nature of assessment between and within subjects was perceived to vary, then variation in approach towards a task was described. Such a *strategic approach* was adopted to attain differing task requirements. It involved the pupil in defining these demands, and in making a conscious effort to vary his methods of studying to achieve the demands, as the above description illustrates.

The investigation has shown that senior pupils do perceive contextual differences between study tasks. Also, that pupils strategically vary their approach to studying accordingly. An important message for classroom practice is that how teachers teach and assess will influence pupils' approach and the qualities of the learning

Table 2.4 Consistency and variability in pupils' approach to specific tasks between subjects

Pupil	Reading	Writing	Notemaking	Problem solving	Practicals
1	S1(G), S1(Ge)	D2(G), D1(Ge), D1(Ec)	D2(G), S3(Ec)		
2	D2(H)	D2(H), D2(G), D3(F)	S3(H), S3(G), S3(F), S3(M)	D2(M)	
3	D2(B), D1(G), D1(E)	S2(B), D2(G)	S2(B), S2(G), S3(E)	D2(B)	S1(B)
4	D1(H), S2(E)	D1(H), D1(E), D2(G)	S3(H), S3(M), S2(E)	S1(M)	D2(G)
5	D3(C), D2(M), D1(E), D2(B)	S1(C), D2(E), S1(B), D2(G)	D3(C), S3(M), S3(E), D2(B)	D3(M)	S3(C), S3(B)
6	D3(E)	D3(E), D3(F), D2(G)	S3(F), S3(M), S3(E), D1(G)	D3(M)	
7	D2(G), D1(E)	D1(G), S1(F), S2(C), D1(E)	D1(G), S3(M), S3(F), S2(C)	S1(M)	S3(C)
8	D2(B), S2(G)	S1(B), S3(G)	S3(B), S3(G)		S3(B), S3(G)
9	D1(P), D3(C)	D2(P), S2(C)	D1(P), D3(C), S3(M)	S2(P), S2(M)	S1(C)
10	S1(C)	D3(P)	S3(P), S3(C), S3(M)	S1(C), S2(M)	S3(P), S3(C)
11	D3(C)	D3(P)	S3(M), S3(C), D1(P)	D2(M)	S3(C), S3(P)
12	D2(B), D3(C)	D2(B), S2(P)	D1(B), S2(C), S3(P)		S3(B), S2(C), S3(P)
13	D2(Ec), D1(E), D3(M), D2(G)	D2(Ec), D1(E)	D3(Ec), D3(G)	S2(M)	S2(M), D1(G)

Key: S1–S3 and D1–D3 = approach subcategories; bracketed P = Physics, C = Chemistry, B = Biology; M = Maths, E = English, attained. Teachers have, therefore, an important role in openly teaching study skills so that pupils are aware of and practised in the strategic control of their approaches to studying. Furthermore, if this study skills teaching is to be effective, the everyday teaching pupils experience must not prevent such flexibility – reliance on formal teaching methods and closed assessment is counter-productive.

The teaching–learning process

This chapter has laid to rest the notion that teaching and learning are synonymous activities. It is upon this received wisdom that much of present teacher training and school practice are organised. Yet it has been shown that the bringing together of a teacher and a pupil of suitable 'ability' will not necessarily yield the desired learning outcome. Rather, teachers and pupils are active partners in a web of relationships within the teaching–learning process.

Perhaps the most important influences a school and its teachers have upon a pupil's learning are in providing appropriate provisions to foster pupils' skill in learning and in the use of appropriate teaching and assessment methods. To complete our understanding of what studying involves, Chapter 3 investigates the nature of study tasks pupils are required to undertake.

3

The Demands of Study Tasks

To put into practice the new perspective on the teaching of study skills, two aspects require understanding. The ways in which pupils undertake tasks were discussed in the previous chapter. Senior pupils will adopt a deep or surface approach to a specific task according to their perception of the situation in which they performed the task. The approach they adopt will in turn affect the potential outcome of learning. So if the learning is to be successful, the approach adopted must be in tune with the demands of a study task. What then is the nature of these task requirements that secondary school pupils experience?

In seeking a reliable answer to this fundamental yet rarely asked question, the view from both sides of the experience should be considered. In designing tasks, teachers should make clear what the precise demands are – the purposes and expected outcomes of the task within a scheme of work. Yet, in spite of such a definition of the teacher's purposes, the pupils' perspective on the context in which a task is performed will determine how it is undertaken. It is, therefore, very important to be clear how everyday classroom tasks are perceived by teachers and pupils.

The evidence about task requirements across the school curriculum is derived from two sets of interviews.[6] Ten experienced teachers from three Edinburgh schools were each asked about the tasks pupils would have to undertake and how they would be organised to master the requirements of the syllabus they were teaching. These syllabuses were O level or O grade (14 to 16 year-olds) and A level or Higher grade (16 to 18 year-olds). The pupils interviewed in the study described in Chapter 2, were also asked about the tasks involved in studying each of the forty-six subject experiences they had.

The evidence

There was a notable degree of consistency between subject specialists' descriptions of task demands at each of the external examination levels investigated. Consequently it is possible to provide descriptions of the nature of learning tasks pupils would meet across the school curriculum. Furthermore, teacher and pupil perspectives of these tasks showed that there was much agreement between teachers' intentions and their classroom activities. Nonetheless, the teaching methods of some teachers, and the type of assessment used in some subjects, did open a gap between the formal aims and pupils' experiences of a task. In such circumstances pupils would have been encouraged to use an inappropriate approach to learning and would have been less likely to attain the learning outcome the teacher had hoped for.

The most convincing evidence is often that which we can judge for ourselves. The three most common tasks across the curriculum were said to be notemaking, reading and writing. Each of these will be considered in detail, using the teachers' and pupils' descriptions. Later on the demands of these and other study tasks will be analysed in terms of deep and surface approaches to learning.

Notemaking

I dictate a very formalised note. I don't want them to have what I feel is extra, unnecessary, stuff in their notebook. And I concentrate on important key words, and phrases and I divide it up carefully into sections.

At O grade, if there's a central issue at stake, then I would give them a detailed note on it.

I always think of it in terms of their memory . . . I mean some of them are able to store vast amounts of information.

At the O level/grade stage the teachers interviewed exhibited a broad consensus. Notes would be structured and their precise content would be provided by the teacher. This content was said to be restricted to the facts with the need to recall in mind, perhaps to meet examination requirements. Even when the process was more of a dialogue between class and teacher, the structure called for uniformity and the teacher maintained overall control:

> Quite often we talk about a suitable framework and I get someone in the class to volunteer a title for the main thing and then get other pupils to identify what would make suitable subtitles . . . I suppose I am telling them what to make notes about.

In studying A level and Higher grade syllabuses, teachers described a more independent task whose content should derive from a variety of sources and need not always be concrete and factual. The integration of information, ideas and views was said to be required. These comments were typical:

> The main noting can come from the lesson and discussion surrounding the lesson. Then perhaps they could read through bits that are different or supplement what I said on bits that I never covered at all.

> We hand out a note which tells them to look up and make their own notes. They are told where to look up the examples.

Some pupils studying these syllabuses did describe making notes in their own way, though what the notes were to be about tended to be defined by their teacher. Pupils related material from a variety of sources, organised how the material was to be structured and tried to involve their own ideas. But at other times they became dependent on the teacher for structure and content when notes were dictated, duplicated or written on the blackboard. The contrast in situation and activity is well illustrated by the following descriptions:

Interviewer: And these notes, are they ones that you make?
Pupil: No. In general we get given duplicated notes and have to copy them out.
Interviewer: Word for word?
Pupil: Or adding in bits if you want. In Chemistry I haven't actually done much extra notemaking.

Interviewer: Have you any other sorts of writing to do?

Pupil: There's writing in that you have class notes . . . You're given notes in class and you either write those out as you're given them and if you don't have time for that, take shorthand notes and after class . . . getting notes from reference books, a diagram here, and piecing them all together.

Reading

Reading was said to be a task required in all subjects. At O level/grade, teachers conceived it like this:

Well, as far as the reading goes, we work very much from one textbook, or maybe two at the most, and we concentrate on small sections at a time.

I try to encourage them to do quite a lot of reading from newspaper cuttings that I've photocopied.

I will set a class specific reading tasks which back up what we've done in the lesson and follow that up with some sort of test as to how well they've grasped what they've read.

Usually, I suppose there is a pattern in the questions I ask in that most of them are factual recall . . . at the end there would be other questions of a broader nature, maybe asking them for their own ideas, opinions, thoughts.

Reading at this level was of texts chosen by the teacher, often as a precursor to a demand to answer questions. These questions commonly sought facts, although they could also extend what pupils already knew and understood.

Despite teachers still tending to direct pupils towards certain texts beyond O level/grade, the demands of reading were said to be more sophisticated.

Normally I would issue textbooks to be read through as a supplement to notes that come up in class.

The O level concentrates on the texts themselves and very little commentary on the text. While at A level you are asked to go to particular critics . . . go out, do research on their own, pick up books on the works, extract useful information.

. . . not just the historical background this time, although I would expect this, but the interaction between different subject areas, different topics, I would expect them to glean from the textbooks.

We might do Rostow's theory – a theory of development – and I would ask them to go and find a situation which you think corresponds to the theory we've talked about in class.

Senior pupils were expected to integrate findings from a variety of sources, searching for ideas or principles and to apply them in a personal manner.

The pupils themselves perceived the task of reading in much the same way, irrespective of the subject. Their conception of reading was also similar to that of the teachers. The task was often experienced as a means of fulfilling other tasks such as notemaking or written exercises. It was an integrative task with the purpose of deriving understanding from the material, as this pupil explained:

Well, basically it is to remind us of what is written in the notes and to get a different explanation . . . Sometimes, you know, the notes will try and explain something in one way, the book will try and tackle it in a different way and the two combined methods will give you a better understanding altogether.

Writing
In the task of writing, other than notemaking, the type of instruction was described as influencing the demands of the writing. The types of instruction used by teachers were said to be determined by those found in external examinations. At O level/grade there was general agreement on the following characteristics:

When we first come across essay planning I will explain it blow by blow because they won't have had to do any.

Writing a paragraph in their own words using a word which we've talked about in a previous lesson . . . using the word correctly in one sentence and elucidating further on by example.

In the end it comes down to, a great extent, memory; the extent to which they simply remember they would use this particular word in this particular context.

The writing would concern concrete, factual and restricted situations, demanding the recall of information. Though the teachers provided guidance on what to write, the degree of pupil participation at the planning stage was much higher with certain teachers:

Interviewer: What do they do in deciding what to write?
Teacher: Well, we spend quite a lot of time talking about that. I get them to take a felt tip pen and underline what they consider to be important and what words and phrases or ideas they would consider worthwhile writing down . . . then we talk about it and compare what they've underlined with their neighbour's underlining and try and see if there is a pattern. Then they would be allowed to write it up, having talked about what we think is important.

For those pupils studying A levels or Higher grades, teachers again described a qualitative difference in the task demands:

I think it is far more the case at A level that you don't actually need to know quite so many facts and there are not so many facts that are necessary ones. It's rather that when you write an essay on a topic, you are selecting from a range of materials – a certain amount of information that is both accurate to the [subject] and accurate to the argument that you are putting across in your essay.

There is a certain amount of factual recall. Pupils have to recognise the concept or the topic which it's about and they're probably expected to define a word at the beginning of a question, and to develop a theme, and then maybe to apply it to a new situation.

Pupils would be expected to use their background knowledge and find their own sources of information. They would have to organise their own written content to apply accurate facts and personal views in a case study or an argument.

Another study of writing across the curriculum in Scottish schools[11] came to a similar conclusion. Though there was considerable variation in the amount and type of writing expected at O grade, writing was mostly a means of storing information for revision and assessment. It was orientated to syllabus content. Pupils who moved on to study Higher grades found the new demands in writing a shock.

Senior pupils interviewed about their writing all considered that the content should be gleaned from a variety of sources, often involving a personal search. They had also found that in some contexts the task was 'open' – enabling a variety of responses – and in others it was 'closed' – demanding only a single correct response. The latter, with purely factual content, tended to be associated with science subjects. The former were linked to language and social science subjects. Their content was more open to interpretation and personal viewpoint. Descriptions such as these were commonplace:

> Well the question was about waves and I looked up in a book what it was actually asking about . . . and then looked at my notes on the subject and then wrote down a kind of amalgamation of the two.

> I took this [essay title] and thought about having a robbery in a bank. As I was thinking about it, I took notes of the introduction . . . have a dramatic beginning . . . and then build up the story, have a middle and then an end when the whole thing's over. Then as I am writing it in full hand I might make side notes as I think of anything extra I might put in later on.

Readers may like to consider the nature of the study tasks that are typical of their own subject and teaching practices, and to explore with pupils how they perceive what is required. Variations amongst pupils will inevitably be found, although broad similarities with the tasks described above would also be expected.

Study tasks across the curriculum

In the previous chapter the concept of deep and surface approaches to learning was developed to describe how pupils performed tasks of studying. The same language can be used to describe the nature of these tasks, both as intended by teachers and experienced by pupils. This background knowledge will provide the basis for reconsidering how study skills ought to be taught in schools.

The interviewees' descriptions were analysed by comparison with characteristics which illustrate a pupil's deep or surface approach towards a task. Distinguishing characteristics include the level of dependence; an aim of personal understanding or passive memorisation; concentration on meaning or fact; and treating phenomena as integrated or isolated. In addition, comments were interpreted in terms of the broader sense of the concept – indications of intention or efforts to interact with the material of a task, or merely to fulfil a task.

Study tasks met across the curriculum were of six types. Notemaking, reading and writing were said to be the most common tasks. Numerical problem solving, investigations by experiment or project, and tasks of remembering, were also mentioned frequently. The characteristic demands of these tasks are illustrated in Tables 3.1 and 3.2. Once again, readers can judge the reality of these descriptions by comparing them with their own experience and practice.

In the O level/grade phase the tasks were described overwhelmingly to demand a surface approach. Pupils' activities were said to be dependent on the teacher for guidance; were generally confined to the facts or concrete situations; memory of these was often required, mostly by unthinking repetition, with the aim of being able to contend with assessment demands; materials were also often treated in isolation from other materials. Aspects of a deep approach were apparent in some tasks. Such characteristics were, however, only described by individual teachers. Situations in which an O level/grade pupil might be expected to adopt such an approach to learning would therefore appear to be very limited across the curriculum.

Teachers felt that the move to studying A levels or Higher grades involved a significant change in formal curriculum demands. For the most part, tasks were described in terms characteristic of a deep approach. Pupils were expected to take greater responsibility for organising and performing learning tasks, with varying incidence of teacher guidance. They were expected to think about contributory concepts and ideas; to concentrate on understanding phenomena; to integrate them and to relate them to their own ideas. Where vocabulary or illustrative quotes were required, they were to be learnt by active and thoughtful repetition to incorporate them into

Table 3.1 Teachers' descriptions of study task demands

Approach / Characteristics	Curricular tasks					
	Notemaking	Reading	Writing	Problem solving	Investigations	Remembering
S dependence	0	0 *	0 *	0 *	0	0 a
U isolating		0		0	0	
R memory task	0	0	0	0	0	0 a * b
F fact task	0	0	0 *			0 0 a
A aim to perform	0			0		0 a
C external motivation	0		0	0		0 a
E						
D independent	*	0 *	*	*	0 *	0 a *
E personal interaction	*	*	*	*	0 *	0 a *
E understanding aim		*	*	0 *	*	a *
E integrative task	*	0	0 *			*
P conceptual task	*			*		0 a *
relativistic	*	0 *	*			*

Key: 0 = 0 level/grade; * = A level/Higher grade; a = unthinking repetition; b = thoughtful repetition

Table 3.2 Pupils' descriptions of study task demands

Approach characteristics		Notemaking	Reading	Writing	Problem solving	Investigations	Remembering
S	dependence	*		*		*e	*a
U	isolating		*	*		*e	
R	memory task	*	*	*	*	*e	*a/b
F	fact task		*	*			
A	aim to perform						
C	extrinsic motivation						
E							
	independent	*	*	*	*	*p	*b
D	personal interaction	*	*	*		*p	
E	understanding aim	*	*	*	*	*p	
E	integrative task	*	*	*	*	*p	*b
P	conceptual task		*		*	*	
	relativistic		*			*	

Key: * = A level/Higher grade; a = unthinking repetition; b = thoughtful repetition; e = experiments; p = projects their previous understanding. Surface approach characteristics were not considered appropriate for any complete task, but were for certain aspects of a task – mostly when a teacher defined exactly what was to be done, but not how. Other aspects of the same task were said to require a deep approach. The use of deep and strategic approaches to learning tasks across the A level and Higher curriculum would appear to meet the teachers' professed demands of studying.

Thus far the task descriptions are probably familiar, but do pupils have similar perceptions? Pupils studying these syllabuses did not tend to see each task in isolation. Frequently one task, say reading, was described as a means to completing another task, perhaps writing or notemaking. Table 3.2 shows that task demands were sometimes perceived to require a deep approach and sometimes a surface approach.

In all tasks, pupils thought they were to integrate materials from a number of sources, be it in constructing notes, researching the content of a written answer or project, or applying what was known about a numerical problem to other similar ones. In some tasks pupils felt they were required to relate their experiences, ideas or imagination to other materials, and even to develop personal interpretations. In some tasks they also felt expected to think about the meaning of materials or to organise the structure of the task.

However, there were contexts in which the teacher was said to determine the structure and content of tasks experienced in the classroom and so to redirect pupils' approach to them. These situations included occasions when notes were dictated, instructions on experimental procedure were duplicated, reading was directed towards specific facts in isolation, factual tests were set, techniques were repeated frequently, and when narrow time restrictions were imposed. Such experiences of some teachers' chosen classroom activities were said to foster a surface approach of passive dependence on the teacher and so led to an intention to memorise material.

Other contextual influences described by pupils were concerned with the intrinsic nature of tasks and possible differences between subjects. Perceptions of open tasks of writing or investigative projects were linked to characteristics of a deep approach. Such tasks were described within language and social science subjects.

Closed tasks were linked with surface approaches and were mostly described for science subjects. Remembering by contextual rote learning was also described within science and language subjects. Then knowledge rather than understanding was perceived as an acceptable outcome for teachers and external examinations. A surface approach alone was considered sufficient for such tasks.

Having been articulated, these factors' influence and the range of differing activities they foster should be readily recognisable. The pupils' experiences complement and extend the description of these task demands established from the teachers' perspective and provide a firmer basis for developing appropriate study skills teaching.

A summary

Learning in schools is organised and experienced in the form of study tasks. Though each task can be seen in isolation, it is also part of a sequence whose structure ought to lead to predetermined learning outcomes. It is the perceived demands of a study task that precipitate a particular approach to learning and, thereby, the quality of learning that might be achieved. In other words, the outcome of learning depends on the nature of the task set, and how the task has been perceived by the individual pupil.

This chapter has compared teacher and pupil perspectives of tasks met across the curriculum. A large measure of agreement between teachers' intentions and the experience of their classroom activities has been apparent. In studying O level/grade syllabuses, tasks almost exclusively require a surface approach. A level and Higher grade syllabuses demand much more of a deep approach, with any rote-learning requirement being limited to particular activities within an overall deep approach. However, the teaching methods of some teachers and the nature of assessment used in certain subjects caused pupils to perceive the need for more strategic studying (a greater variation of approach, as explained in Chapter 2) than teachers described.

The implications are two-fold. The factors which affect pupils' approaches to learning are now more clearly understood. Thus a conscious effort to equate teaching methods with the professed aims of a task should become necessary characteristics of effective and professional teaching. Moreover, a full description of pupils' approaches and the nature of the tasks they are required to undertake provides a sound basis for deciding what constitutes appropriate study skills teaching.

PART THREE

How should Study Skills be Taught?

4

Learning How to Learn

The previous chapters were concerned with the background to study skills in secondary schools. The need to teach study skills has been established and yet fundamental weaknesses in conventional assistance have been identified. One such weakness involved the 'best method' nature of advice when teachers' experience and research evidence both suggest that successful learners work in different ways. Another weakness was the failure to relate study skills assistance to the task demands that pupils actually experience. The research project which was introduced in the previous chapters indicated the nature of pupils' study tasks and how they go about their studying.

In the final part of this book, attention is turned towards how these insights might be applied within secondary schools to enhance pupils' learning skill. The nature of what can now be considered appropriate study skills provisions are discussed in this chapter. An illustration of a coherent course developed from this basis is presented in Chapter 5, while the evaluation of the impact on pupils' learning is considered in Chapter 6. The implications for the entire school experience, of educators acquiring an understanding of the dynamic nature of the teaching–learning process, are pursued in the final chapter.

The research findings described in Chapters 2 and 3 showed that learning involves an active partnership between teacher and pupil. In this partnership teachers plan the demands of individual study tasks to meet wider educational objectives. A pupil's perception of these demands affects the approach to learning adopted and, thereby, the potential outcome of that learning. If, however, pupils do not develop conscious control over how they undertake tasks, the learning is less likely to be effective, despite the teacher's organisation. Pupils need to learn how to learn. Teachers and schools ought to actively encourage this process.

The curriculum demands of A level and Higher grade syllabuses have been described by teachers and pupils as requiring independence and the strategic use of approaches to learning (see Chapter 3). In studying syllabuses for younger and less academic pupils there might not be a demand for strategic approaches to learning, but there is still no case for prescribing how a task should be done. It was shown in Chapter 2 that, even for the same task, different strategies suit different individuals and the same individual in different situations. It would, therefore, be in the short and long-term interests of all pupils to have practice and encouragement in thinking about how they carry out study tasks. The prescriptive teaching of supposedly 'good' study methods derived from didactic 'cookbook' advice can no longer be justified. So what type of assistance could be considered appropriate?

The general principles

The new perspective on the teaching of study skills is based upon an understanding of the learning process in schools – an understanding which emphasises the interaction between teacher and learner illustrated in the research evidence of Part Two. To guide pupils in learning how to learn they should be encouraged to play an active part in their learning. To develop the necessary skills of independence and control over their learning process, pupils need:

1 *to think about their learning* – to be helped to become more aware of what they do and to evaluate the effectiveness of their own studying;
2 *strategy practice* – assistance to accumulate a range of strategies to apply selectively to the perceived purpose of a task.

Alongside these principles, there are further aspects which are likely to be advantageous in assisting pupils to learn how to learn. In the review of the study skills tradition in Chapter 1, it was found that few pupils realised they had received any assistance, and those that did realise found difficulties in applying that advice within their normal work. The advice lacked relevance, cohesive structure and reinforcement. As a consequence, pupils also need:

3 to see relevance in the advice through practical exercises which focus on the types of task pupils actually experience in their everyday studying;
4 opportunities to reflect on their learning through a set of concepts and ideas – a language – which describes the processes of studying; and
5 to apply their new found study skills in situations similar to those in which the skills were initially learned and across the curriculum. Initial reflection on approaches to studying may be stimulated through a general course, but there will always be a need for follow-up across all subjects.

The rest of this chapter is devoted to suggesting the type of activities which could be used in normal classes to apply these general principles.

Up to 16 years old

Most pupils' experiences of lessons in the lower school are of teacher-dominated and subject-centred teaching. This was certainly how teachers described the demands and organisation of study tasks in O level and O grade syllabuses (see Chapter 3, Table 3.1). The restrictive form of examination questions, voluminous syllabuses, an emphasis on fact rather than understanding, and the perceived need to pass on the accumulated knowledge and values of society, each contribute to such narrow formalised teaching. But it also occurs because of a lack of attention to how pupils learn.[11]

The consequences of such teaching are fundamental to pupils' experience of learning. Subject-centred teaching concentrates exclusively on the finished product: the notes made or the exercises written. Supposedly 'objective' marks can then be given. Yet facts tend to change rapidly; subject experts and society rarely agree on what information and values are important or even true. Organised in a restrictive, dependence-forming manner, only the limited learning outcomes associated with a surface approach to learning can be expected (see Chapter 2). Even these might be developed at the expense of increased frustration and boredom with the subject.

Why then are such experiences of teaching and learning common-place? What might be done to balance the subject-centredness with appropriate help in learning how to learn?

In Chapter 1 it was suggested that teacher training practices may, in part, be responsible for the lack of appropriate study skills assistance. With the focus of initial training upon the presentation of a subject's content, the skills of learning tend to be ignored. Furthermore, teachers beginning to teach study skills are, inevitably, uncertain of their knowledge and expertise in the area. Publications which provide 'firm' knowledge are found to be comfortable. The review of conventional study skills assistance in Chapter 1, showed how the inappropriate impression of 'best methods' contained in study skills cookbooks is then reinforced by the teaching methods adopted.

Up to approximately age 16, descriptions of the demands of learning across the curriculum were found to involve tasks mainly confined to concrete situations and the recall of information (see Chapter 3). Pupils' activities were firmly controlled by the teacher and the demands of learning could be met by a surface approach (see Chapter 2). However, this does not imply that a uniformity of approach should be encouraged. Such uniformity in study strategy was not found to characterise an individual pupil's studying let alone that of all pupils. Also, with the studying of a subject being part of the broader educational objective of personal development, narrow prescription of study strategy cannot be justified. If pupils are to be interested in and challenged by their studying, and if they are to acquire the skills of learning, they also need to be guided to think about and to monitor how they undertake tasks. The research findings also indicate that new skills require practice. This takes time which has traditionally been filled with subject content. Opportunities for practice within everyday studying depend on the active support of subject teachers who are conscious of learning processes and organise their lessons accordingly. How, then, can these two main principles be translated into practical classroom exercises in the years leading up to the first external examinations?

Thinking about learning
The first principle of appropriate study skills assistance is to help pupils become more aware of what they do and to evaluate the

effectiveness of their studying. To begin with, this guidance is inevitably time-consuming, but it will pay dividends. In the early stages it is particularly important to allow time for pupils to make and reflect on 'honest' failures, which make the later performance of a task all the easier. With such efforts in all lessons, pupils come to understand what works for them, and time will be saved later on.

In Part One the need for a language for considering the learning process was identified. The potential gap between 'knowing' and 'doing' induced by the presentation of 'ideal' characteristics was also discussed. The following activities concern these aspects and form a basis for pupils' reflection on their learning process:

Activity A:
There are three considerations in the thoughtful performance of a task (see 'Flexible advice' in Part One; Harri-Augstein *et al.*;[23] Nisbet and Shucksmith)[33]. These are to ask:

1 What are the goals or purposes of the task?
2 How might these goals or purposes be achieved (the strategy)?
3 What qualities are required of the final piece of work and have they been achieved (a review of the outcome)?

Each of the aspects could be discussed with pupils in relation to specific tasks undertaken. They provide a structure for assessing learning.

Activity B:
In responding to the range of possibilities in the self-questioning exercises of Figures 4.1 and 4.2, pupils' attention can be focused on their thoughts and actions concerning a task. The 'purpose' exercise could be completed and discussed before the task is carried out. The 'strategy' exercise could be used retrospectively to establish the success of using a particular strategy to meet a certain purpose. The teacher need not be involved in the discussion immediately, small groups of pupils being capable of reaching conclusions when provided with clear instructions. A teacher might prefer to discuss the findings with each group of pupils. The conclusions of all the groups in a class could then be brought together to highlight the variety of strategies which achieve a specific purpose. Pupils who have employed a strategy which did not attain the purpose may then have another attempt at the task.

Figure 4.1 A self-questioning exercise about the purpose of a task

Here is a list of reasons why a piece of writing might be done. Tick the reason(s) why this piece of writing is being done:

Reasons for Writing	√
1 To help learn something by writing it down.	
2 To show the teacher what I can do.	
3 To have something to revise from.	
4 To practise for an exam.	
5 To show the teacher what I have remembered.	
6 To work out what my ideas are.	
7 To put something into my own words.	
8 To have a record of what I've done.	
9 To help me learn how to write.	
10 To help me fit together new facts or ideas with other facts or ideas I already know about.	

Figure 4.2 A self-questioning exercise about strategy

When you were doing this piece of writing, what did you do? Tick the box(es) that best describe what you did.

Did you:	√
1 Identify the most important points and write those down.	
2 Copy the facts out word for word.	
3 Write the information in your own words.	
4 Use the special way of writing required in this subject.	
5 Summarise information.	
6 Record, report or describe events.	
7 Record or describe information.	
8 Present evidence and draw conclusions.	
9 Report or describe something and make your own judgement of it.	
10 Try to persuade someone of your point of view.	

Figures 4.1 and **4.2** are adapted from exercises produced in the Scottish Council for Research in Education's Writing Across the Curriculum project (Spencer, 1983a, 1983b).

Activity C:
The consequences of certain actions can be investigated by provoking discussion and decision-making in response to a cartoon or diagram which illustrates these actions. Pupils faced with the compounded incompetence of Disaster Dave (Figure 4.3) are unlikely to be alienated in the way supposedly 'ideal' characteristics might. All pupils can feel superior, even if they identify with some features of Disaster Dave. They can discuss how the problems arise and what they would be to avoid getting into these difficulties. Pupils could be asked to keep a record of the difficulties they get into. These might then be used as stimuli for discussion in a subsequent lesson.

Figure 4.3   The Saga of Disaster Dave (from a course on planning and organisation developed at George Watson's College, Edinburgh)

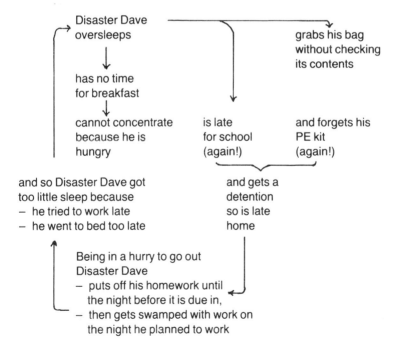

Strategy practice

The second principle of appropriate study skills assistance is to help pupils to practise a range of strategies and to apply them selectively to the perceived purpose of a task. It was shown earlier in the chapter that such practice ought to focus on the type of task pupils actually experience in their everyday studying. Also, that practice should take place in normal lessons even when a general study skills course is experienced. The activity suggestions below, cause pupils to think about what they do, to consider the purpose of a task, and they also provide practice in using strategies. They reflect the reality of studying at this level in that the nature of the tasks is defined by the teacher (see Chapter 3). However, in promoting the need for pupil's independence in how tasks are undertaken, 'best method' strategies are not prescribed. Whether prior to experiencing a task or in gaining practice within a general course or a subject lesson, discussion of thoughts and actions is encouraged. Sharing ideas and reaching personal decisions through discussion can be a valuable means of learning to learn. There is often a strong feeling among pupils that finding out what others do is cheating – a consequence of competitive assessment within formal methods of teaching. Through discussion, pupils are led to see that they can learn from each other's attitudes and experiences.

Activity D:

Discussion about how a task might be carried out can be useful before the task is actually met. This is especially so for revision and assessment tasks. By introducing a parallel situation, pupils are provided with something specific to consider and to compare with their own past experience of similar tasks. The importance of planning before doing tasks is then emphasised and decisions can be made about how the task is to be approached. (This activity is adapted from D. Hamblin, *Teaching Study Skills*, Basil Blackwell, 1981.)

1 Organise a discussion acted out between two pupils comparing their revision strategies.
2 Explain the situation to the other pupils in terms similar to those they face themselves; for instance, the pupils wish to revise for their end of term examinations a fortnight ahead. They have certain decisions to make, namely:

– how long will a revision session last?
– will breaks be taken?
– if breaks are to be taken, when and for how long?
– what activity will be involved?

3 The two actor/pupils, presented with a short script drawn up by the teacher, are overheard discussing how they intend to organise their revision. One intends to do some each day, perhaps an hour at a time. The other prefers to make an evening of it, lasting possibly two or three hours, with a short break every half-hour. The first pupil thinks a break of five minutes attractive. They mention that they will end by a few minutes spent in testing themselves: one with a tape recorder to record what is recalled, the other using a diagram. Both describe making notes during the revision: one intends to use record cards, the other uses file paper.

4 Divide the class into small groups (3–5 pupils) for discussion of what strategy they think is best for their own revision, guided by the decisions to be made. Suggest that each pupil describes their decisions and justifies them to the others in the group.

5 End the session by suggesting that their chosen strategies are tried out that evening and that a report on their experience is made the next day.

Activity E:

Strategy practice can be encouraged within the context of a specific lesson. If a particular body of information has to be recorded, decisions have to be made about how to treat the material. Pupils could be asked to suggest different forms of presentation and these can be discussed. Suggestions might include continuous prose, paragraphs with headings, flow diagrams, tables, divided circles, cartoons or even film scripts. Having discussed the possibilities, each pupil can be responsible for choosing how to present the information. The products can then be viewed and their success in portraying the information discussed. Provided the teacher does not become an arbiter of taste, pupils may be helped to understand how information can be recorded effectively. (This activity was suggested by Rosemary Hector, formerly of The Edinburgh Academy.)

Activity F:
Attention can be focused on goals and actions in studying through formal practice of a strategy which is then discussed and applied to a real learning task. The purpose is to *identify* separate issues within a text and use them as a basis for a *summary* of the text.

1 Teacher to select a source or sources of information involving separate (though possibly connected) issues.
2 Explain to the pupils that they are going to practise a way of summarising information contained in a piece of writing.
3 Instruct pupils to highlight/underline and label sections of the text with headings decided by the teacher in advance (e.g. one label for a paragraph's meaning or more labels for sub-sections as appropriate).
4 Ask pupils to highlight/underline and make headings of their own for other parts of the text.
5 Encourage the pupils to compare and discuss their headings in pairs or small groups.
6 Point out to pupils that they have the skeleton for a summary of the information. Ask them to write out the summary in their own words.
7 Pupils should be set a summary exercise as part of their normal learning. (This activity was adapted from materials produced by teachers to help teach study skills in the SCRE project, Spencer, 1983a and b.)[11]

If pupils are to become skilled learners rather than classroom automata, it is vital that they are encouraged to think about how they study long before they are required to be fully independent of their teachers. Teacher directed training in study skills ought to begin in the younger age groups in secondary school. It should become an integral part of normal lessons, provoking renewed thought whenever new tasks and situations evolve. Such guidance would be self-defeating if it were prescriptive. The activities described in this section give some ideas about how study skills can be taught appropriately within the early and middle years of secondary school. They can be adapted to suit the particular situation within a school or lesson. The dividends of such assistance are in providing solutions to the weaknesses of teaching and learning that research has shown to be commonplace at this level. Teachers can become more responsive to the learning process and pupils can be provided with regular opportunities to think about and practise their developing skills of learning.

At 16+

When pupils continue their education into 16+ syllabuses they begin a completely new set of experiences. Whether or not they have received study skills teaching in previous years, the demands of learning they experience come as a shock.

> They find it very difficult to understand what is required of them
> . . . and they find it difficult over a two year period to amass the
> skills necessary to enable them to meet the demands of their
> subjects independently.[13]

If pupils' learning is to be effective and stimulating then it is important that study skills form a component of their studies, in a form that will help them meet the demands they face. With different demands of learning, assistance will necessarily be different from that provided for younger pupils.

The research evidence in Part Two of this book has shown that senior pupils are expected to take more responsibility for organising their own learning. Teachers and pupils described studying at this level as involving ideas and experiences as well as information, collated from various sources, the focus being on meaning and understanding – characteristics of the deep approach to learning identified in Chapter 2. Yet with teachers structuring lessons and setting tasks, and with the need for certain information to be learnt before it can be applied, the demands of a task were not always the same as the demands of a syllabus. Pupils found that, at times, a surface approach would suffice (see Chapter 3). So pupils need to be guided towards recognising the different approaches required, identifying the demands of a specific task, and adopting appropriate strategies. Pupils have to be strategic in their approach to studying. To be independent, they also have to discover which strategies work for them.

The most fundamental consideration for teaching study skills at this level is the creation of opportunities and time for pupils to think about what they do. The influences on the approach adopted, described in Chapter 2, showed that restrictive contexts cause anxiety and an intention to memorise materials (a surface approach) whilst less restrictive contexts allow a search for understanding (a deep approach) to take place. Thus teachers who act on a compulsion to spoonfeed information, who view an unsuccessful task as a reflection on their teaching rather than a learning event in its own right, who fear failure and so compel pupils to do things their way, whose lessons are always hurried, and who see exams as the only end product of learning, will fail to create these opportunities. When there is conflict between the rhetoric of curriculum demands and practice in the classroom, pupils will not learn how to learn. Nor will they be able to meet these demands using their full potential.

For the appropriate teaching of study skills at 16+, teachers' attitudes and practices developed over many years may need to change. The dread of an uncompleted syllabus should be seen for what it is, a view of learning as gaining knowledge rather than understanding. Anxiety about independent-minded pupils being disruptive or asking awkward questions is understandable but ought to be resisted. Inertia and reliance on teaching methods which create dependence are not the marks of an effective professional. Curriculum demands and teaching practices must coincide. At 16+, pupils need to develop the capacity for independent and strategic studying. Few can do this without guidance from their teachers or without the freedom to explore their own learning strategies.

An understanding of the teaching-learning process at 16+ suggests, therefore, that the aim of study skills teaching should be to enhance an independent and skilled approach to studying which strategically relates strategy to purpose. Unlike the guidance for pupils up to 16 years old, the general principles of thinking about learning and strategy practice need to be combined. This could be done through activities which encourage thought and provide practice in relating purpose, strategy and outcome – the three fundamental considerations in carrying out a task.

Where the assistance should also differ from that provided for younger pupils is in the nature of the tasks considered and in the onus on each pupil to decide what works for them.

An introductory course followed up by subject specific guidance within each subject is one approach schools might adopt. The alternative is coordinated action by individual teachers across the

curriculum. The general principles of appropriate assistance indicate a need to guard against a provision that is seen to be detached
from pupils' normal work; a special, once and for all time, course on
study skills. Applicaton of what is learned to real study tasks would
then be most unlikely. Assistance ought to be sustained throughout
a course, fostering reflection about the study process, and be of
immediate application.

What sort of activities, then, are appropriate in teaching study
skills to senior pupils?

Self-assessment of work
Evaluation of a pupil's own work can stimulate an appreciation
of the processes involved in undertaking a task. Self-assessment
schedules stimulate a pupil to think in detail about their learning
purposes, strategies and outcomes. They can provide a description
of current practice and a platform for change towards effective
strategies in fulfilling particular purposes. Furthermore, in
assessing completed assignments, pupils can learn to anticipate the
sort of observations teachers might make about their work. Thus
pupils can be assisted to control the quality of their work before it is
formally assessed.

Activity G:
Ask a pupil or pupils to complete a self-assessment schedule, along
the lines of that shown in Figure 4.4, with a recently completed piece
of work in mind. Use this as a basis for discussion with the pupils
about the qualities of the assignment. Alternatively, divide the class
into small groups (3–5 pupils) and ask the pupils to compare their
work and responses with that of others in the group. Strengths and
weaknesses in undertaking the assignment can be identified. In
organising their next assignment pupils could be encouraged to bear
these findings in mind.

Activity H:
1 Give pupils a copy of a completed assignment (a newspaper
   article, prose written by a pupil or in a textbook, or a speech) and
   tell them what the purpose of the assignment was.
2 Ask pupils to read/listen to the completed assignment and to note
   how the assignment was organised to achieve that purpose.

Figure 4.4 A self-assessment schedule (adapted from D. Hamblin, *Teaching Study Skills*, Basil Blackwell, 1981).

1 *Preparation*
Did you accurately identify the purpose or purposes intended by the instructions?

2 *Planning*
Was your work adequately planned? Was the content relevant? Did you relate the task to previous work?

3 *Presentation*
Does your intended meaning get across to a reader of your work? Does our conclusion derive from the evidence presented? Were the relationships between aspects shown clearly?

4 *Outcome*
Did the finished product achieve the intended purpose(s) of the exercise? If not, what were the weaknesses in your work?

5 *Change in your strategy*
In performing the same or a similar exercise in the future, what changes would you try to make in how the exercise is carried out?

3 Repeat for other completed assignments with similar or different purposes, making notes on each one.
4 Consider with the pupils how each purpose was achieved.
5 Give pupils a copy of another completed assignment, asking them

to read/listen to it, identifying how it was organised and, from this, what the author's purpose was. Discuss the pupils' findings.
6 Provide pupils with copies of other completed assignments, mentioning a purpose for each which may or may not have been achieved by the assignment. Ask pupils to assess the quality of each assignment in respect of its stated purpose, writing comments about and giving a mark to each assignment.
7 Encourage pupils to swap their assessed assignments, to compare and discuss their assessments until they understand each other's comments and marking.
8 End the session by pointing out that this experience of the assessment procedure could be applied directly to work a pupil is about to undertake.

Structured group discussion
When pupils have a number of years' experience of learning, they do have a background to share in discussion. In structured group discussions the teacher provides structure and materials, while the pupils experience a common task individually and discuss their attitdues and approach to it in increasingly large groups. Everyone is encouraged to participate. Teachers might define the purposes to be considered and suggest strategy possibilities. Prescription of strategy would, of course, not be appropriate. Varieties of strategies for individual tasks can then be exposed, together with the effectiveness and appropriateness of each for the particular purpose of that task.

Activity I:
(This is an adaptation of activities suggested in G. Gibbs, *Teaching Students to Learn – A Student Centred Approach*, Open University Press, 1981.)

Working individually:	Presented with a short text, tape or video-recording, pupils are asked to make notes about what they see or hear.
Working in pairs: (5–10 minutes)	Pupils are asked to study each other's notes; to find out what is similar and what is different about (a) how the notes are organised, and (b) what is included in the notes.

Working in fours: (10–15 minutes)	Pupils are asked to study each other's notes as before; and, for each set of notes, to decide what purpose such notes would be best suited to achieve (e.g. for a factual test, a summary, the content of an essay).
Working as a class:	The spokesmen for each group of four pupils are asked, one at a time, to describe a purpose and a type of notes that have achieved this purpose (an OHP copy of these notes would help a description). Pupils from other groups may be asked to suggest other types of notes which can be useful for the same purpose. Continue until discussion or time runs out.

In each of these activities it is the pupil's responsibility to consider the relationships between purpose, strategy and outcome, and to derive personal conclusions about a task. They can be adapted to suit particular situations met by pupils in a school or lesson or in private study. (Further exercises are included in Chapter 5.) In such activities the teacher acts as the facilitator, concentrating pupils' attention on these aspects of the learning process. In this way pupils can be helped to monitor their own studying. The desirable skills of independence and a strategic approach to learning are thereby fostered.

A whole-school policy

Many teachers and schools are already convinced of the need for pupils to learn how to learn.[33] Earlier chapters have laid out a sound basis for deciding what are appropriate means of teaching study skills in secondary schools. A new perspective was found to be necessary and this chapter has sought to provide some guidelines for action – essentially to encourage reflective attitudes towards studying based on the identification of purpose and strategy, followed by an evaluation of the outcome in relation to the purpose. The teacher and pupil descriptions of study tasks in Chapter 3 showed that the need to control how one learns is not limited to certain subjects. Teaching study skills ought not, therefore, to be the concern of a restricted group of teachers. A whole-school policy is what is really needed.

The traditional didactic, authoritarian style of teaching has been shown to be inappropriate for developing pupils' skill and interest in learning, and for achieving the professed demands of studying. Similarly, the educational organisation of school life into discrete subjects without a unifying theme is likely to fail to create learning which pupils can readily apply beyond the school context. However, with schools actively encouraging pupils to learn how to learn, improvements in the effectiveness of, and satisfaction with, learning in secondary schools would be expected. The independence fostered and the practice in being strategic would also help later activities in higher education, work and leisure. What then, would a whole-school policy involve?

As this chapter has already indicated, pupils should be encouraged to take increasing responsibility for their own learning. This would require their active involvement in the learning process, together with a critical awareness of how they carry out study tasks. The previous chapter gave evidence of how learning demands change as pupils move through secondary school. They need to receive sustained, appropriate and evolving assistance that will lead to independence at 16+. Active consideration of how to learn ought to be a part of curriculum planning. Coordination of aims and methods between teachers of each subject and between departments is, perhaps, the key. The isolation of mechanical skills within each subject would be broken down. Pupils could then monitor the purpose, strategy and outcome of study tasks they experience in all subjects, not just the subject content. They would then be learning in a skilled and self-motivating manner.

How would all this fit into present school practices? There is, after all, a good deal of inertia in this area. Many teachers have yet to be convinced of the desirability of teaching study skills. Even for those who have already been persuaded, in the past the appropriate approach has been far from clear. Any initiative has to overcome the hurdles of bulging syllabuses, full timetables, teachers under pressure to get pupils through examinations, and the numerous curriculum developments that already absorb teachers' free time.

Introducing 'learning to learn' activities is likely, therefore, to be a gradual process, but it should not be protracted. With the full support of a head teacher, a group of committed teachers within a school could initiate activity and develop materials in collaboration with subject departments. A general course would probably have an important role at this stage. In providing a basis for the teaching of study skills, trial and evaluation of the materials might persuade more teachers of their value. Familiarity with the aims, materials and teaching methods could then be disseminated systematically. Heads of department or principal teachers' meetings, departmental meetings and in-service sessions might become the focus for further developments. In this way, study skills could gradually become a part of normal lessons. A whole-school policy would have evolved. But its success would inevitably depend on a developing acceptance of the importance of systematically helping pupils to become skilled learners.

It may well be that the introduction of a general course is the best way to interest colleagues and pupils in the importance of learning how to learn. The next chapter describes the details of such a course which was developed by the author and taught, with colleagues, at Merchiston Castle School in Edinburgh.

5

Learning to Learn Materials

The new perspective on the teaching of study skills introduced in this book depends on a recognition that learning involves a partnership between teacher and learner. It also involves a conscious recognition of the importance of relating the purposes, strategies and outcomes of study tasks. It seeks to shift the focus in teaching as a whole, from subject content alone, to include the process of learning. The basis for this new approach is research evidence of how pupils go about their studying and of the nature of the tasks they are required to undertake.[6,30] This indicated that pupils need to be aware of, and to exert control over, their own study activities. As a consequence, they would be more able to overcome their learning difficulties, and might be more interested in their learning. In Chapter 4, guidelines were introduced for appropriate study skills assistance within normal class teaching in secondary schools. This chapter builds on these guidelines to present the rationale of, and materials for, an integrated course for pupils at 16+.

The research project described in Part Two of this book found that, in studying A level and Higher grade syllabuses, pupils used both deep and surface approaches to learning. When faced with a study task their choice of approach was determined by their perception of the context in which the task was experienced. Influential factors were the methods of assessment, the formality of the teaching, a pupil's dependence on the teacher, and the time available (see Chapter 2). Both teacher and pupil perspectives of the 16+ curriculum described pupils' independence and the need to strategically employ contextually variable approaches to specific tasks (see Chapter 3). The previous chapter's guidelines for appropriate assistance suggested, therefore, that study skills teaching at this level ought to concern the whole study performance -- to foster awareness of, and practice in, relating purposes, strategies and outcomes of study tasks.

A skilled learner is able to transfer ideas and practices learned in one context, to other similar contexts. Learning in school is experienced through study tasks and some of these tasks are met across the curriculum (see, for instance, Table 2.4, page 28). For pupils to see relevance in study skills teaching, and to help pupils to transfer their skills between subjects, the general principles of appropriate assistance included the need for guidance to be organised around the tasks experienced in everyday studying (see Chapter 4). Note-making, reading, writing and revision (active remembering) were four of the most common tasks pupils experienced (see Chapter 3). The course described in this chapter focuses on these tasks.

For pupils to reflect on their learning, the general principles of appropriate study skills teaching suggested they would require a framework within which to think and organise themselves (see Chapter 4). The mnemonic **PSR** provides such a framework. It relates to the fundamental characteristics in the thoughtful performance of a task (see Chapters 1 and 4): **purpose** refers to the pupil's perception of the aim and importance of a specific task; **strategy** relates to how the task is organised and carried out; **review** involves identifying the outcome of using that strategy and checking it against purpose to decide whether or not the task has been completed successfully. In the course described in this chapter, familiarity with the framework is developed by relating its aspects to pupils' attitudes and experiences concerning organisation of studying in general and the four common study tasks. Thus the course has five exercises.

Each exercise in the course contains a description of the aims, teachers' notes and the activities involved. In organising the course in such a fashion, a certain standardisation of presentation and activities is ensured. These then conform to the guidelines for 16+ assistance developed in the previous chapter, whoever teaches the course. The teacher's role as facilitator rather than prescriber is also protected. In keeping with the activities suggested in Chapter 4 as being appropriate, the exercises centre around the experience of a shared task undertaken near the start of a session. Individual experience is shared by discussion, sometimes in small and at other times in larger groups. However, if all pupils are to be encouraged to contribute, experience indicates that total class sizes should be kept below twenty. Thus pupils are exposed to a repertoire of strategies towards a task, together with the effectiveness and appropriateness of each strategy for various purposes of the task. At the end of each exercise the teacher provides a summary of the decisions reached and pupils keep the worksheets as a reminder of what has taken place. In this way the process is investigated in a personal, practical and transferable manner, derived from an understanding of the learning process.

The materials presented in this chapter could form an introduction to study skills at 16+. But a general course cannot stand on its own. Versions of each task experienced in each subject of the curriculum cannot possibly be included. Such a course ought to be conceived as part of a more general policy, preferably a whole-school policy (see Chapter 4). The exercises below also provide a basis for adaptation within normal subject lessons.

TOPIC 1:

Thinking about learning

From the outset, self-monitored studying requires a framework and a language with which to work. In the following exercise **PSR** is introduced – standing for Purpose, Strategy, Review. It is applied to pupils' feelings about their organisation in studying, guided by clear instructions and worksheets that focus on common organisational problems (see Chapter 1). The exercise begins to make discussion of studying socially acceptable. It is, after all, something that few pupils otherwise discuss, with the strong social pressure to give an outward appearance of casualness. The sense of such co-operation is not lost on those involved, as this pupil acknowledged after experiencing the course:

> I think it's only when you get a course like this that people talk about these things. I think people try and lock them up and they don't talk about what the purpose is or they don't talk about what the possibilities [of a task] are. They think it's cribbing or something. If we talk about it, it would be much easier instead of making a problem of it.

Exercise 1

Aims:
- to raise awareness of the importance of organisation;
- to focus on strategies that foster organisational attributes;
- to introduce a structure for thinking about organising one's learning (PSR).

Time needed: 30–45 minutes.

Teachers' Notes:
In introducing the course the teacher might stress the following:

- Most learning tasks in the lower school have been organised by the teacher but pupils are now expected to take more responsibility for their own studying.
- Success in school and afterwards will depend largely on how well pupils adapt to new situations. In this course the aim is to start everyone thinking about *how* they study and learn, to help gain control of it.
- How organised learners are is the one aspect of studying that consistently correlates highly with academic success. Well-organised pupils do better.
- Many difficulties arise from a *passive* approach, starting with no clear purpose in mind, concentration drifting at every potential distraction. What must be borne in mind is that studying is an *active* process, involving *thinking* about what one is trying to do and *organising* a strategy to the task.

Activity:
1 Teacher should compile a Worksheet along the lines of Figure 5.1 and consult it with the rest of the class. Ask pupils to read the statements, ticking those that seem to apply personally and altering others to make them do so.
2 Divide the pupils into small groups (3–5 pupils) in which to compare their responses, giving the following suggestions verbally and in writing:
   (a) Compare your responses to each statement.
   (b) Decide whether each statement matters when studying.
   (c) For each statement your group feels matters, share ways in which you may have overcome the situation.

Figure 5.1 Worksheet 1: Organisation

How organised you are is the one aspect of studying that consistently correlates highly with academic success. Well-organised pupils do better. How organised you are and changing how organised you are involves, more than any other aspect of learning, your feelings.

Read the list of situations below which you might experience in your studying.
Tick those you feel apply to yourself.
Alter the situation statements so that they apply to you rather better.

1 I often seem to leave things such as essays and exercises to the last minute.
2 I am often late in handing work in.
3 I seem to work better in some places than in others.
4 I'm never quite sure what I've got to do next.
5 Fairly often I put off planned work until another day.
6 I am not all that prompt in starting work.
7 There are many distractions where I do most of my work.
8 I am easily disheartened by studying.
9 I am forever chasing about after things I need to study.
10 I often seem to run out of time when studying.

A group leader should be appointed to take notes. Allow up to 15 minutes.

3 Compile and consult a Worksheet along the lines of Figure 5.2. Point out that when thinking about *how* we learn we can organise our thoughts to consider Purpose, Strategy and Review (PSR). It is a summary of an active learning process.

Define each term:

Purpose   =   what the aim of a task is, why it is important;
Strategy   =   how the task is organised and carried out;
Review   =   identifying the outcome of using that strategy and checking this against purpose to decide if the studying has been successfully carried out.

4 All groups now share their earlier discussions.

Take one small group at a time and one statement they thought important. The first group should tell the others why the situation mattered (P), how it has been overcome (S), and the outcome in comparison to the purpose (R) of using that strategy.

Figure 5.2 Worksheet 2: Thinking About Learning

| PURPOSE
Your aim/task importance | STRATEGY
What you did | REVIEW
Did the outcome from using this strategy attain your purpose? |
|---|---|---|
| | | |

The teacher should structure each group's conclusions in terms of PSR, on a blackboard/OHP, with pupils entering relevant points on to the Thinking About Learning Worksheet. Encourage discussion. Repeat for other groups and other statements, with pupils making their own notes.

5 Summary. Point out that to study effectively you have to think actively about what you do. This may be done using PSR. This mnemonic will be met in the later task-related exercises of the course.

TOPIC 2

Reading
The use of printed materials to gain knowledge and understanding is part of studying across the curriculum. To help pupils gain control of

this task there is a need to be conscious of their own particular difficulties. Focus is also brought to the fact that a pupil does read in different ways; that these should relate to the purpose of the task; and that there are a variety of strategies that people use to attain the same purpose, whilst certain strategies are unlikely to be effective for particular purposes. Pupils' understanding of the dynamics of reading is strengthened.

Exercise 2

Aims:
- to develop an awareness of personal difficulties in reading;
- to develop an awareness of purpose in reading;
- to provide practice in relating strategy to purpose;
- to consider the effectiveness of reading result in relation to purpose.

Time needed: 45 minutes.

Teachers' Notes:
In introducing this exercise the teacher might stress that:

- printed materials are a major source of knowledge and means of understanding in all subjects, so the effective use of books, journals, magazines and newspapers is of immense importance in studying;
- most people experience some difficulties in reading effectively;
- difficulties in using printed materials often stem from a passive strategy with no clear purpose in mind. What pupils need is active thought about what they are trying to achieve (purpose), and of how to attain that purpose in reading (strategy);
- the result of reading needs to be reviewed to see whether they have been effective in attaining their purpose (review). If not another strategy ought to be used.

Activity:
1 Compile and consult a Worksheet along the lines of Figure 5.3. Each pupil should respond to the instructions on the sheet.
2 Conduct a brainstorm of purposes in reading and produce a note on the blackboard/OHP. (Purpose might include: for pleasure; to identify main points; to summarise; to get the gist; to criticise; to find the author's message, etc.)

Figure 5.3 Worksheet 3: Common Reading Difficulties

Read the list of common reading difficulties below which you might experience or have experienced in the past.
Tick those statements you feel apply to yourself at present.
Alter the other statements so that they apply to you rather better.
If you experience any other reading difficulties then add them in the space(s) below the other statements.

1 I quickly forget what I have read.

2 Reading is boring/sends me to sleep.

3 Finding the author's main points is difficult.

4 I often have to read something many times.

5 I read everything in the same way.

6

7

8

Point out that if there are various purposes then it is logical that there should be different strategies for reading.

3 Consult a short article chosen by the teacher from a textbook or journal which pupils might use in their studying. A suitable article would contain a reasoned argument or contention and would be readable within five minutes (such as Appendix 2A, page 108). In pairs, ask one of each pair of pupils to read the article to themselves with the purpose of 'assessing the strengths and weaknesses of the evidence' and to make a note of these. Ask the second member of each pair to read the article with the purpose of 'identifying the main points made' and to note these down.

Each pupil should then complete the appropriate sections of a Worksheet along the lines of that shown in Figure 5.4.

4 In groups of four, including an appointed chairman, ask pupils to

Figure 5.4 Worksheet 4: Active Reading

ARTICLE	PURPOSE	STRATEGY	REVIEW

share their experiences of reading the article, giving these guidelines:

(a) Compare the notes arising from reading the text with the first purpose in mind; discuss the strategies used and their effectiveness in meeting this purpose.

(b) Compare similarly for the second purpose.

(c) Complete the Active Reading Worksheet.

5 Debrief on the Active Reading Worksheet. Focus on one purpose of reading the article at a time. Ask individual pupils to describe how they undertook the reading (strategy) and how effective this had proved to be in achieving the purpose (review). Summarise the strategies which were found to be effective in attaining each purpose considered.

6 In the same groups and, using a Worksheet similar to that

shown in Figure 5.3, ask pupils to compare and discuss their difficulties, how they arise and how they might be overcome, noting conclusions on the worksheet.
7 Summary. Remind pupils of the use of PSR in reading as an active way of organising reading tasks. Point out that with different purposes in mind, different strategies ought to be used if the purpose is to be achieved.

TOPIC 3

Notemaking
Being one of the fundamental tasks of independent learning, the making of notes is a common source of difficulty in studying. On the other hand, gaining control of this task can give a major sense of achievement and competence, as this pupil realised:

> Before the course I didn't like studying and I didn't like notemaking. As I didn't like notemaking, I didn't really like school. But after the course I liked notemaking. I enjoyed making my notes and other people wanted to look at my notes. Since then I enjoyed them . . . because I could do them better and could do them easier. I got better marks and enjoyed the process of work.

Once again, co-operation and pupil's own experiences are the basis for enhancing thought and action on this task.

Exercise 3

Aims:
– to consider the variety of purposes in notemaking;
– to practise making notes to suit a particular purpose;
– to raise awareness of the variety of notemaking strategies;
– to consider the notes made in relation to the purpose of making them.
Time needed: 45 minutes.

Teachers' Notes:
In introducing this exercise the teacher might stress that:

- making notes is a very common task in all subjects;
- notes are important to make because they are a storage mechanism for facts, ideas, theories, relationships, experiments, experiences and views, so that they can be used later;
- notes are made for one's own use, so it is the pupil who has to decide on the precise purpose in making a certain note;
- once the purpose is known then a strategy can be devised to make the note, i.e. to create a structure for organising the material. The notes produced can then be checked for their usefulness by relating them to the purpose you had in making them (PSR).

Activity:

1 Divide a class into groups, each of three pupils. Each pupil in a threesome is given the same text.
2 Ask each threesome to make notes from their text with each pupil using a different one of the following purposes:
    (a) make a note for revision towards a factual test;
    (b) make a note to contrast the similarities and differences between the examples mentioned;
    (c) make a note to summarise the main points mentioned.
    Allow approximately 10 minutes.
3 Within threesomes, the notes made should be passed around, compared and discussed, with these suggestions given verbally and in writing:
    (a) Identify the similarities and differences in the notes made from the same text but for different purposes.
    (b) Discuss how effective each note is in attaining its purpose.
    Again allow 10 minutes.
4 To highlight the variety of notemaking strategies used, the teacher might ask the class who:
    - produced a longhand (full sentences) note?
    - produced a mini-paragraph type of note?
    - produced a number point note?
    - produced a different type of note? (What type was it?)
    - and whose note attained its purpose effectively?
5 To expose a greater variety of purposes in notemaking and a different strategy, ask for suggestions and build a patterned note on the blackboard/OHP. For example:

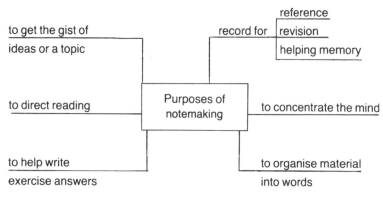

6 Explain that patterned notes are an alternative notemaking strategy, useful for many purposes.

Ask pupils to use the same purpose and text as before, and to make a patterned note.

Threesomes should compare the notes produced as before. Allow 10 minutes.

7 Summary. Point out that pupils ought to use different notemaking strategies for different purposes; that different pupils might choose to use different strategies for the same purpose; that the strategy used produces notes that should suit the purpose they were made for; this can be checked using PSR.

TOPIC 4

Writing

In most subjects written work is the task that forms the basis of assessment. Not only is there considerable variation in the format of the writing that pupils meet, other than notemaking. Individual subjects also have their own conventions. Not surprisingly, writing can be a daunting task if pupils are not in control of how they go about such tasks. Reviews of pupils' study difficulties suggest that common problems concern planning and critical thinking (Table 1.1, Chapter 1).

Exercise 4

Aims:

– to consider how to identify purposes in writing tasks;

– to develop awareness of the purpose-strategy relation in writing tasks;
– to raise awareness and provide practice in the critical appraisal of written products.

Time needed: 30–45 minutes.

Teachers' Notes:
In this exercise the teacher might stress the following:

– Writing is a task experienced in studying all subjects and it is generally the task that is assessed.
– Academic success, to a large extent, therefore, depends on skill in writing.
– Individual subjects have their own conventions for structuring writing – the scientific method for experiments, the introduction and body and conclusions of long essays, etc. Pupils should ensure that their subject teachers make very clear what is required in their subjects.
– In this session the aim is to think about the *content* of writing. In all subjects the written content should vary according to the precise purpose in doing the writing. A strategy should be used which organises the content into a product that attains the purpose.
– PSR can be used to organise one's thinking about writing and can enable everyone to be critical of the writing they produce.

Activity:
1 Compile and consult a Worksheet similar to that shown in Figure 5.5. Point out that for every purpose there are particular writing characteristics required to attain that purpose. The success of carrying out a writing task can therefore be thought about using PSR.
2 The teacher gives an illustration of planning writing:
Ask pupils to read an article or exercise answer (such as in Appendix 2B and 2C, pages 110 and 111) with the intention of identifying the likely purpose of the writing from its qualities.
Ask for a possible title/instruction that could have led to such writing being produced.
Point out that by thinking about purpose and qualities, writing

Figure 5.5   Worksheet 5: Purposes and Qualities in Writing (adapted from E. Spencer, *Writing Matters Across the Curriculum*, SCRE, 1983)

COMMON PURPOSES	WRITING QUALITIES	TYPES OF WRITING READ
1 To show knowledge by describing subject content, perhaps to assist in later recall or revision.	Record of accurate information, ideas, definitions or instructions.	
2 To summarise content or argument.	Identification of the most important aspects – key points.	
3 To explain or show understanding.	Presentation of information etc. in own words; showing the relationships between aspects; making appropriate use of vocabulary.	
4 To develop an argument; present evidence and draw conclusions.	Selection of relevant and important points with illustrative examples; generalisation from detail; statement of implications.	
5 To show personal thought or views; to discuss; to persuade others of a point of view.	As 4 above plus: inclusion of feeling, opinion, experience, and an awareness of other viewpoints.	

can be planned and its success gauged. The style of writing used for one purpose may not be appropriate for other purposes.

3 Ask pupils to read another article and, in small groups, identify their writing qualities and likely purpose. Debrief after 5–10 minutes.

4 The use of PSR to assess the quality of writing:
   Suggest a certain duplicated exercise answer was written in

reponse to a given instruction (such as in Appendix 2D, page 112). Ask pupils to decide the purpose of the writing task, to identify its writing qualities and to discuss these aspects in their small groups, noting conclusions on the worksheet. Then ask each pupil to mark the writing out of 10 and to add their comments.

Discuss and repeat as time allows.

5 Summary. Point out that to develop skill in writing, PSR needs to be thought about. Purpose might be identified from the title (author's purpose) or from instructions (teacher's/pupil's purpose). A strategy needs to be chosen that will produce a product that meets the purpose. This is what a marker looks for and is something pupils can do too. Such thought is needed before actually writing, and afterwards.

TOPIC 5

Revision

All pupils are required to remember certain ideas and information as a background to further study of a topic or subject, or in preparation for examinations. Since few people have photographic memories, revision or active recall is necessary. A pupil has to develop knowledge and awareness of how information is stored and retrieved. Planning ahead is then made possible in selecting and implementing appropriate revision strategies. A key distinction to be made in this selection is between active and passive strategies. Pupils also need to come to terms with their personal difficulties. In sharing their experiences pupils are helped to understand their problems. They are also able to decide how they might become more effective in revising, not by accepting any single 'best' method, but by considering their own and other people's strategies and then by adapting their current procedures. As one pupil said:

> I think that if you get everyone's idea with your ideas and you think 'I've got better ideas than theirs, I'll just stick to what I'm doing myself.' Or, if someone has a better way, you could adopt it.

Exercise 5

Aims:
- to raise awareness of the variety of purposes in a task;
- to consider active rather than passive approaches to revision;
- to focus on pupils' experiences about effective revision strategies.
Time needed: 30–45 minutes.

Teachers' Notes:
In introducing this exercise the teacher might stress:

- When learning, pupils are often required to remember work studied to help in the understanding of subsequent work, for tests and for examinations.
- Pupils will often find that they have to do this for a number of subjects at the same time.
- At the start of the course it was mentioned that many difficulties arise from a *passive* approach. What is needed is an *active* approach involving *thinking* about what one is trying to do and *organising* a strategy for the task.
- Throughout the course PSR has been used to structure an active approach – in other words thinking about the precise purpose, organising strategy and, afterwards, evaluating how effectively the purpose has been met.

Activity:
1 Ask pupils what purposes they may have had in doing revision. The teacher could draw up a patterned note of suggestions, such as:

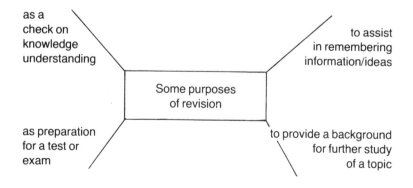

Figure 5.6 Worksheet 6: Revision 1

When revising, you may have one of a variety of specific purposes in mind. An appropriate strategy needs to be chosen if the result of your revision is to be attained in terms of the purpose. Broadly, there are **active** and **passive** approaches to revision (and all studying).

Read the following list of statements about revising.
Classify them into two groups:
(a) those describing active thought and organisation
(b) those describing passive approaches.

Statements	*Group*
1 In my revision I try to summarise the topic.	.....
2 During revision I concentrate on one point at a time.	.....
3 When revising I concentrate on learning the facts.	.....
4 When trying to remember something new I link it to something I already know.	.....
5 I revise things by saying them over and over in my head.	.....
6 When revising I concentrate on what I don't know.	.....
7 When revising I consider how the various aspects link together.	.....
8 I try to memorise everything when I revise.	.....

Point out that with different revision tasks having different purposes, a variety of strategies need to be considered.

2 Compile and consult a Worksheet similar to that shown in Figure 5.6.
Ask pupils to read the statements, classifying them into two groups:
(a) those describing active thought and organisaton;
(b) those describing passive approaches to revision.
(answers: a = 1, 4, 6, 7; b = 2, 3, 5, 8)

Debrief, asking why.
Allow up to 15 minutes.

3 Compile and consult a Worksheet similar to that shown in Figure 5.7.
Ask pupils to read the statements, ticking those that seem to apply personally and altering others to make them do so. Add others if necessary.

4 In small groups (3–5 pupils, one acting as chairman), responses should be entered using these instructions:
   (a) compare responses to each statement;
   (b) for each statement, discuss how the situation arises and share ways in which some pupils have overcome the situation, making notes on the Revision 2 Worksheet.
Allow up to 15 minutes.

Figure 5.7 Worksheet 7: Revision 2

REVISION STATEMENTS	STRATEGIES USED TO OVERCOME THE SITUATION
1 I find it difficult to revise things I studied a long time ago. 2 I find things I didn't understand originally difficult to revise. 3 Subjects with a lot to revise are a problem for me. 4 I don't find enough time to revise as much as I need. 5 I tend to get muddled when revising topics that are similar. 6 When revising I have difficulty in recalling the exact words used. 7 After revising something I tend to forget it quickly. 8 Often, I don't know whether I have revised a topic adequately. 9 10	

5 The whole class should now share their discussions.
Take one group at a time and one statement. First group should tell the others how the situation might arise and how they have tried to overcome it.
Open the discussion to others' experiences.
Encourage pupils to make further notes on the worksheet.
Repeat with other groups and statements.

6 Summary. Point out that revision is a very common study task, just like notemaking, reading and writing. In all tasks it is necessary to think actively about, and to organise one's studying. Studying may be controlled by using PSR to think about *purpose* in a task, to select and apply a *strategy*, and to *review* the outcome in terms of achieving the initial purpose. If the purpose has not been met the task has not been completed effectively and requires another attempt, using another strategy.
PSR can be applied to help pupils undertake study tasks in an active manner.

6

Evaluating the Experimental Course

The last two chapters have considered the nature of appropriate study skills' provisions at different stages of the secondary school experience. Guidelines for, and illustration of, exercises in learning how to learn have been suggested. From these, readers might adopt or adapt as is felt to be appropriate to meet the needs of their pupils. Fundamental to this new perspective on the teaching of study skills has been an understanding of how pupils go about their studying and of the nature of the tasks they are required to undertake (described in Chapters 2 and 3 respectively). In completing any innovation there is one more step that should be considered, namely evaluation.

If the appropriate teaching of study skills is to become an accepted part of teaching and learning in schools, then evaluating of any experimental course is vital. Merely creating a course does not guarantee that its aims will be achieved. There may be aspects which require improvement, deletion or addition. If developments are to be seen to be relevant and useful then colleagues need to be able to judge this for themselves. The impact on how pupils study and on their attitudes to learning ought to be established.

In this chapter, three means of evaluating an experimental or pilot course will be considered: by questionnaire, interview and inventory.

Questionnaires

As the aim of teaching study skills is to affect pupils' thoughts and actions in the way they learn, it is the pupils themselves who should be asked about the experience. Perhaps the quickest means of doing this, and of asking large numbers of pupils, is the self-response questionnaire.

Using the same set of questions, everyone is asked exactly the same things and the responses are directly comparable. Statistics are readily built up. On the other hand, the rigid form of the questionnaire may constrain individuals' responses and there is little scope for probing the answers. Since the purpose of an evaluation is to discover pupils' attitudes, a series of conventional YES/NO answers is not really subtle enough. However, if the questions are open-ended, then they are difficult to analyse. The design of a questionnaire needs careful consideration if it is to achieve anything useful.

A means of discovering pupils' feelings and opinions, and yet easing the analysis, is to ask a direct question and supply a choice of replies. For example:

How confident are you in organising your studying? (Underline your view.)
very   fairly   slightly   barely   not at all

But in order to uncover reasoning behind a reply, then space must be provided for explanation, just enough for a summary. For instance:

Have you found that the way you study has changed since the course?
YES/NO
If YES, explain in what way it has changed:

Certainly, questions should be phrased in such a way that all pupils will understand them. Anonymity may also have to be ensured if pupils are to indicate their real attitudes.

A self-response questionnaire that follows these simple but effective guidelines is shown in Figure 6.1. It could be used to evaluate the Learning to Learn course described in Chapter 5. Questions ask about the application of aspects met in the course, about the way it was organised, about its overall usefulness and about any changes which might be suggested. All valuable information for improving and justifying a provision.

Figure 6.1 A model for a questionnaire

Learning to Learn Course: Questionnaire

You can help to improve the studying course that you experienced recently by answering the following questions and offering comments.

Your course consisted of these exercises:

1 Thinking about Learning
2 Notemaking
3 Reading
4 Writing
5 Revision

....

Q.1 Which of the skills dealt with have you found difficulty with in the past? (ring exercise numbers)

    1   2   3   4   5   none

Q.2 Which of the skills dealt with have you used since the course?

    1   2   3   4   5   none

Q.3 Which of the skills are you likely to make use of in future?

    1   2   3   4   5   none

Q.4 Are there any other skills you would have liked to find in the course? If so, outline:

Q.5 What was your opinion of the following aspects of the course.
(a) the worksheets?

(b) the discussions?

(c) PSR (purpose – strategy – result)?

Q.6 Was the overall course: (underline your view)
too short   adequate   too long

Q.7 Did you find the course: (underline which)

very helpful   helpful   neutral   unhelpful
very unhelpful

THANK YOU FOR YOUR HELP

Valuable data might also be obtained from questionnaires completed by teachers involved with teaching study skills, and from parents. If interest is shown then inquisitiveness and support are often forthcoming.

Interviews

The perceptions of those experiencing assistance can also be tapped by interview. The personal nature of this technique means that it is adaptable to the individual and it is easier to discover what a pupil really thinks. In this respect the interviewer needs to be on guard in case a pupil feels that there is a response the teacher would prefer to hear. By stressing that it is what the individual pupil thinks which is of interest and by allowing pupils to respond without interruption, interviews can provide insights that are otherwise unobtainable.

There are a number of potential difficulties. Interviews take a long time. Consequently only a small sample of pupils can be interviewed. If the sample is to be representative of all pupils experiencing a provision, then a cross-section will have to be identified. This might be every nth name in a list of those involved, or equal numbers of each sex and class. The larger the sample, the more reliable the data, but with the law of diminishing returns having its effect, the interviewer will have to judge when to stop. Pupils may have difficulty in describing how a task is carried out. As with the interviews described in Chapter 2, the presence of material used or produced during a recently performed task will assist such a description. It is also important that the comments made can be compared between interviews. Thus a note of pupils' replies ought to be taken, with a full note of any particularly interesting comments. Recording of interviews might help if fuller investigation were thought to be necessary. Also, the meaning of questions asked should be kept constant in all interviews, though the phrasing may be varied to suit the individual circumstances. Such consistency will be made easier by designing an interview schedule, such as Figure 6.2, before the interviews commence.

The value of interview data has already been seen in the pupils' observations included in Chapter 5. The impact of words is often more immediate than that of statistics. If responses only describe

Figure 6.2 Semi-structured interview schedule

Usefulness of exercises:

Q.1   You seem to have found exercise X of the course useful in your studying. Would you tell me how you made use of it in a particular piece of work.

Q.2   You said that you have found exercise Y of the course to be of little use in your studying. Why do you think this is so?

Q.3   Are there any other tasks you would have liked to have seen included or left out in a future course?

The course structure and methods:

What is your opinion of:

Q.4   the worksheets?

Q.5   the discussions?

Q.6   the mnemonic PSR?

Overall impact on studying:

Q.7   You have said that you found the course .... Would you explain why?

Q.8   Has the way you study changed as a result of the course?

the acquisition of tips for studying, then it will be apparent that a more fundamental awareness of the learning process has not been achieved. Alterations to the guidance would then be called for. However, if the aim of appropriate study skills teaching had been met, then some comments would be more like the ones obtained from interviews with pupils who had experienced the course in Chapter 5:

Pupil: Before, in a bit of work you were given you didn't really know the point to it, and you can see as you get gradual success that there is a purpose to it. You feel a lot more confident in it. You can only really start to build up success with building blocks and then build upwards. Before, I sort of had an apathetic view to it, you just had to do it.

Interviewer: Has the way you study changed as a result of the course?

Pupil: Yes. In the way I've gone about things. In the way I've thought about things. It's actually changed the results I get . . . I think about it now.

Pupil: The course was helpful but it didn't change the way I studied. It made me think more clearly about what I was studying.

Improvements in confidence, competence and understanding about how studying is performed are what is being sought. Descriptions such as those above, and those included in the introduction to certain topics of the course in Chapter 5, might be seen by colleagues to justify the inclusion of a study skills provision in a school's curriculum.

Interview data can be of further value in that opinion is expressed about how the study skills assistance has been organised. With this knowledge, decisions can be made about which aspects are in need of revision and on the nature of the changes required. The usefulness of particular aspects of the provision may also be highlighted, as was the case with the following comments made by pupils in the author's evaluation:[6]

Interviewer: I wonder what your view of these worksheets was?

Pupil: Well, I thought they were the great thing about the course. If you don't do worksheets or things like that, it's taught theoretical, the mind just drifts. When you have a worksheet you sort of concentrate on it more. There would have been something lost if they weren't in. It would have just been another course. It's something practical.

Interviewer: What about small group discussions, how did you find those?

Pupil: They were probably more productive because you had the points from four or five people. You had everyone contributing. It's often that you get people who don't want to say out in class, but if they can say it in a small group of other pupils then, you know, it is useful, you get other opinions.

Interviewer: Within the course, running through it, there was a mnemonic PSR; I wondered what your view of that was?

Pupil: I thought it was a handy thing to have in that one can go to an essay and say, 'What's the purpose of it?' You locate the purpose. Then you say how you're going to attack it. I mean, if you don't do that you have a terrible attitude to it, of: I've got to do it and there's no purpose in it . . . I use it quite often . . . it can be quite interesting.

In the interviews carried out with pupils who had experienced the course in Chapter 5, persuasive evidence was also obtained about the need to go beyond an introductory study skills course. Pupils felt that there was a need for more help in how to learn within normal subject lessons, as one pupil explained:

Interviewer: Do you find there is any help given in your normal lessons, in how to study?

Pupil: Not really, because most teachers seem to be doing their best to get through the course and to, well, make sure you understand the stuff and teach the material to you. So not many teachers do consider that aspect . . . Surely there must be ways, within each subject, of learning and studying particular to that subject!

Evaluation by interview is, therefore, capable of providing a depth and breadth of insight into the experience of study skills assistance which is unobtainable by other means. If improvements are to be made to an experimental course, if its impact on pupils' learning is to be identified, and if colleagues are to be able to judge the value of teaching study skills in appropriate ways, then interviews have an important role to play.

An inventory

Pupils may indicate a use for aspects of study skills assistance on a questionnaire, they may even describe the application of critical self-monitored studying in certain tasks, but has their approach to learning actually changed? Does the provision cause an increase in independence and use of a deep approach by senior pupils, to balance their former reliance on surface approaches? One way to find out is for pupils to complete an inventory.

An inventory consists of a series of questions to which respondents indicate the extent of their agreement, usually on a five-point scale, each point having the same meaning for each question. The questions are extracted from the empirical basis of the concept to be tested (in this case, approaches to learning and the influences upon them), and are grouped into scales by factor analysis of the responses from pilot surveys. Questions with similar meaning are thereby grouped together. Responses to each question contribute to scores on each scale, changes in which become apparent with subsequent uses of the inventory.

The Studying At School Inventory (SASI), to be found in Appendix (page 101), can be used to describe and to measure changes in a pupil's approach to study tasks and related study attributes. It was developed out of the research findings described in Chapter 2,[6,30] which also formed the basis for the course described in Chapter 5. Its five scales refer to:

S1 : deep approach
S2 : surface approach
S3 : organisation
S4 : motivation
S5 : hard work

The 57 questions are paraphrases of pupils' descriptions of how they undertake studying, including those described in Chapter 2. They were selected from an original 222 questions by factor analysis, which also indicated how to divide the questions to form scales which provide scores on each aspect of studying. (Details of the factor analysis, also the reliability and validity of the inventory, are to be found in Selmes, 1985.) The final questions represent the most cohesive descriptions of each scale's meaning. In the first two scales, the twelve questions apiece refer to each of the three categories of deep or surface approach (see Chapter 2) and to the four common study tasks included in Chapter 5's course. Organisation also relates to these tasks. Motivation describes both intrinsic and extrinsic forms. The fifth scale, hard work, describes pupils' attitudes to putting effort into studying.

A pupil responds to the inventory by circling a letter out of the selection of A to E beside each question, according to the strength of their agreement with the statement.

A = always or almost always true
B = generally true
C = don't know or impossible to decide
D = not so often true
E = rarely or never true

Scoring of a pupil's responses generally takes the form of 4 to 0 for circling an A to E respectively. Letters are used instead of numbers to avoid pupils making conscious attempts to core highly. For the same reason some of the questions are stated negatively and the normal scoring scheme is reversed (i.e. 4 to 0 for E to A respectively). Furthermore, questions on each scale are dispersed randomly throughout the inventory and their scales are not indicated. Scoring, therefore, requires a score sheet to identify each question's scale and score direction (this is also shown in Appendix 2). Total scores on each scale are out of 48, except for scale 5 which is out of 36.

The impact of a study skills provision on pupils' approach to learning can be judged by each pupil filling in the inventory before the provision and at a later date. Changes in the scale scores represent the impact. However, it ought to be realised that the passage of time, other school experiences, individual maturation and health, all have an influence on a pupil's studying.

The inventory could also be used to establish a pupil's approach characteristics and so to identify possible weaknesses in an individual's learning process. Appropriate study skills assistance might then be provided, taking the form discussed in earlier chapters.

Table 6.1 Scale score profiles using The Studying At School Inventory (SASI)

Group	n	deep approach S1	surface approach S2	organisation S3	motivation S4	hard work S5
School A	55	29.6	31.9	25.4	32.1	21.6
School B	45	30.8	28.4	26.4	28.0	22.1
School C	40	28.2	26.8	25.5	26.2	20.4
All schools	140	29.5	29.0	25.8	28.8	21.4
Pupils						
W		23	31	26	32	22
X		29	30	22	29	20
Y		33	27	26	27	23
Z		26	24	27	20	21

NB   The SASI is to be found in Appendix 1, page 101. The scores for the schools are mean scale scores.

In illustration of such a use of the Studying At School Inventory, data might be examined from 140 pupils who completed SASI before they received any form of study skills assistance.[6] Their mean scores on each scale are shown in Table 6.1. Such measures might be taken as standards against which to compare individuals or changes in an individual's characteristics. Pupils' score profiles, as suggested in Table 6.1, could be interpreted in the following manner:

Pupil W: with high motivation and surface approach scores but a low deep approach score, might benefit from the better awareness of how to control his own studying that a general study skills course could bring.

Pupil X: with a particularly low organisation and hard work scores but standard approach scores, may have a strategic capacity but may not be able to control it consciously; general and subject specific study skills assistance may nurture this potential.

Pupil Y: with strong deep, and weak surface approach scores, may not need further study skills teaching.

Pupil Z: with low approach and motivation scores, may lack an awareness of purpose and confidence to act independently; any study skills assistance would need to focus on these fundamental and personal aspects if more appropriate characteristics are to be learned and applied.

However, it should be recalled that without the appropriate teaching and assessment practices, pupils cannot be expected to develop the appropriate approaches to learning that can enable them to achieve the educational aims of their curriculum.[6,30,32] Too great a reliance on the teaching of study skills in overcoming the shortfalls of individual teachers and schools ought to be guarded against.

Whatever the type of evaluation adopted, it is an important part of any innovation. The identification of strengths and weaknesses can lead to improvement of the provision. To be able to describe the effect on studying is to know how effective the Learning to Learn programme is in achieving its aim. Evidence is also at hand to allow colleagues to judge the value of teaching study skills and to justify its inclusion in the curriculum. The implications of such teaching for the experiences of teaching and learning in secondary school, are the subject of the final chapter.

7

Teaching and Learning in the Secondary School

Teachers today are faced with bulging syllabuses and numerous pressures on their time. Professional training has tended to focus on the content of learning, and there is an ever-rising demand for paper qualifications. In teaching there has thus been a temptation to be didactic and to instil a type of learning which can be readily regurgitated for examinations. The consequences of all this have been far-reaching both within and beyond the school system. In Chapter 1 it was argued that most pupils experience difficulties in their studying but few teachers have been able to provide effective help in how to learn. Where such assistance has been available it has tended to be prescriptive. Some pupils' motivation to learn has been adversely affected. Amongst those pupils who were academic successes at school, some have been found to lose their competence in learning when they leave, finding it difficult to adapt to the new demands of higher education or work. Furthermore, certain employers have complained that employees direct from school cannot apply their learning in ways which are relevant outside the classroom. Yet secondary education need not be so. This book has suggested an alternative approach, one in which the learning process is given consideration alongside the content of the learning. Through the appropriate teaching of study skills it has been shown that there is the potential for a better understanding and control of the learning process by pupils, and for changes in teaching methods which would encourage more active and effective learning.

Study skills have certainly been taught in the past, though more in the tertiary than the secondary sector. But these attempts might be described as 'first generation' innovations.[2] They were usually based on 'cookbooks' whose idiosyncratic 'best method' advice fostered inflexible and dependent study habits; and this despite abundant evidence that successful learners tend to be systematic in adapting their study strategies to the demands of specific tasks. The practical guidelines in this book describe a second generation of innovation. The basis of this new perspective is an understanding of the teaching-learning process – how pupils go about their studying, the nature of the task demands they are required to undertake and the teacher's influence on these activities (see Chapters 2 and 3).

In this final chapter these three aspects are summarised, as are Chapter 4's conclusions about what makes for appropriate study skills teaching. Practical difficulties in introducing study skills to the curriculum and the implications for the entire school experience are then considered.

The empirical background

Senior pupils undertake study tasks sometimes with a deep approach and at other times with a surface approach (see Chapter 2). A deep approach, by intention or action, involves attempts to integrate material personally, to seek relationships between materials, and to extract meaning from the material in a task. In contrast, with a surface approach a task is carried out passively, aspects of the material are kept isolated, and the material is memorised. This language for describing how pupils learn was seen to be readily recognisable from everyday observations in the classroom. It is a realistic and practical description of how pupils study and of the qualities of the learning that might be achieved. Using a deep approach understanding can be developed, but with a surface approach learning is restricted to rote-learned knowledge.

The approach which pupils adopt towards a task after the 16+ examinations depends on their perception of the context or situation in which it is experienced (see Chapter 3). 'Closed' types of assessment, formal teaching methods or those which cause a pupil to be dependent on the teacher, and situations in which time is felt to be tightly restricted, have all been found to push pupils towards surface approaches. The converse of these factors facilitated deep approaches.

Younger pupils, including those studying at O level or O grade, experience tasks which almost exclusively demand a surface approach. Pupils' activities tend to be guided by the teacher, are mostly confined to factual or concrete situations which are often treated in isolation and are to be remembered for subsequent assessment. Tasks at A level or Higher grade do, however, demand much more use of deep approaches and less use of a surface approach. For the most part, pupils are expected to take greater responsibility for carrying out tasks. The aim is to acquire understanding through the consideration and integration of concepts, ideas and information.

Nonetheless, senior pupils' experience of these curricula suggest that greater use of surface approaches is caused by certain classroom activities. Such situations include occasions when notes are dictated, when experimental instructions are duplicated, when reading is directed towards specific isolated facts, when factual tests are expected, when techniques are repeated frequently, and when narrow time restrictions are imposed. When a teacher chooses to use these activities, a passive dependence on the teacher and an intention to memorise materials are fostered. Study strategies and learning outcomes are then diverted from the real aims of this educational stage.

Appropriate study skills teaching

It is not unreasonable to have to learn how to learn. Learning is a skill, possessed by all to some extent and, like any other skill, is capable of being developed. The traditional assault course of trial and error has been ineffective for all but the most able pupils. In Chapter 4 it was suggested that with the better understanding of the process of learning in secondary schools, summarised above, it should be possible to describe the characteristics of appropriate study skills teaching.

The aim should be to develop in pupils a critical awareness of how they study so that they can monitor their own learning activities. As a consequence, pupils are likely to show a greater interest in their studies. Teachers ought to consider being less didactic and think how they might organise classroom activities that foster approaches to learning which can lead to the desired learning outcomes. This could involve a focus on *purposes* in undertaking specific tasks, on *strategies* for carrying them out, and on *reviewing* the outcome of using a particular strategy in terms of the purpose of the task. The mnemonic PSR provides a framework to think about and organise studying. Assistance might also offer possibilities and practice in applying PSR in a self-critical way to tasks experienced in everyday studying; it ought not to be prescriptive.

All pupils in secondary school are likely to benefit from thinking about how they study and being able to take more responsibility for their learning. The nature of the guidance should vary for different age groups, however, reflecting the changing curriculum demands. Up to 16 years old (the English fifth-form and Scottish S4), pupils might be encouraged to think about and decide how they will perform tasks. Carefully structured exercises, taking just a few minutes within a lesson, can help pupils to understand what works for them – how material might be read, organised or presented to achieve a certain purpose. Self-questioning worksheets and dis-cussion are means of sharing pupils' experiences, raising awareness of a range of possibilities and their effectiveness. At 16+, pupils should be encouraged to relate the requirements of the learning situation, or the task demands, to the strategies which might be employed. Pupils could be encouraged to be critical of their own studying and to be so without the constant presence of a teacher, and to transfer ideas or practices met in one situation to other similar contexts. Co-operation between pupils in considering how studying might be done is likely to be beneficial. Specific ideas for exercises to teach study skills at these two levels have been suggested in Chapters 4 and 5.

Study skills ought not to be seen as another subject in the curriculum for, if it is perceived to be divorced from normal classroom practice, the learning is unlikely to be applied to tasks pupils experience in subject lessons. Study skills should be the concern of all teachers no matter what their special teaching sub-ject. Teaching ought to take account of the process of learning as well as what is learned. Furthermore, with learning demands chang-ing as pupils move through secondary school, sustained and evolv-ing study skills assistance would be helpful. Its aims and methods could be co-ordinated between teachers of each age group and each subject, and between departments. Ideally, what is required is a whole-school policy.

Practical difficulties

There is still a need to persuade teachers brought up on the inviolable nature of subject content, that the teaching of study skills is of comparable importance. One difficulty is that innovation is readily interpreted as radical interference with accepted practice and, as such, to be avoided. However, for a number of years secondary schools have been in the throes of adjusting to new syllabuses and assessment methods. Teachers have been in the front-line of curriculum development. In addition, most teachers have shown a willingness to take part in in-service training – discussing new issues, refining their skills and adapting their teaching methods. Ideas on study skills provision should be part of these developments.

Planning a whole-school policy on study skills can provide all the support needed for the innovation – its value being immediately apparent. The development and evaluation of materials for use in different subject lessons may provide a more tangible starting point. From such a beginning familiarity with the aims, materials and teaching methods can then spread. Such strategies might develop alongside in-service sessions concerning the process of learning and the importance of the teachers' influence on this process. By raising interest in and an understanding of study skills teaching, involvement is likely to follow. In the author's experience, teachers who have got this far tend to find that they change the way they teach, that their lessons become more stimulating, their pupils more interested and the learning is altogether more effective. Their experiences can be infectious if channelled within a whole-school policy to place the planning of learning beside the planning of other aspects of the curriculum.

In the longer term, the initial training of teachers should be designed to provide greater opportunity to show initiative and to develop a personal style of teaching. At present, student teachers tend to adopt the teaching methods they experienced when pupils or ones they observed in the teaching practice schools. If they were to learn about the teaching–learning process, their teaching practices might be guided by this understanding and be less reliant on intuition and history.

Certain administrative details can also present difficulties. Time has to be allocated from already tight timetables for any introductory course and in normal lessons for subject-based assistance. It ought to be realised that the time involved is only a tiny proportion of a year's lessons, and through developing more effective learners the exercise becomes time-saving – time is not 'lost'. Staff and resources also have to be made available, in common with all curriculum developments. Departmental meetings, head of department or principal teacher meetings, and in-service sessions can provide useful opportunities to discuss, develop and share ideas and materials. Rooms with flexible seating arrangements are also desirable if pupils are to consider how they learn by working in small groups and as a class. A co-ordinated whole-school policy could make such problems easier to solve.

Persuading pupils to take a more active role in their learning may also be difficult at first. Brought up on a diet of teacher dependency, freedom can be disorientating. Pupils may even still want to be told how to undertake tasks, exerting pressure to return to the familiar routines. This should be resisted. Experience has shown that once pupils are given the opportunity to practise self-critical strategies, and they become accustomed to this demand in their everyday tasks, pupils can become more responsible for their studying.

Some Implications

Schools are for learning. The teacher's role is to help bring about that learning. Institutionalised education is not, however, isolated from the rest of society. The potential for learning and applying that learning also exists in the everyday experiences of living. Yet it is apparent that learning in school and beyond has not been as effective as it might be: many pupils have fundamental problems in performing learning tasks; learning skills are often poorly applied out of the situation in which they were first experienced; and disillusionment with the school system is rife. But crises provide fertile ground for introspection and innovation. The placebo effects of superficial reorganisation are all too common in these circumstances – symptoms of a failure to understand the situation. What is really needed are ideas which are soundly based and capable of improving the school experience. One such concept is the appropriate teaching of study skills.

Pupils can learn how to learn. They can be taught the skills of studying, not in a prescriptive fashion but by creating opportunities for pupils to apply these skills in ways which work for them as individuals. Raising a pupil's awareness of what they do; developing a repertoire of study strategies; and fostering self-monitoring of the learning process (by reviewing the relationships between purpose, strategy and outcome), are as important a part of teaching as is subject content.

To put this into practice, all teachers could consider the educational aims of their school, and the teaching and learning activities that take place in it. At the school or department level, the planning of learning might be integrated with other aspects of management. A whole-school policy, involving all staff and spreading across the curriculum, is one way to co-ordinate thought and action. There may well be a need for teachers and new entrants to the profession to acquire an understanding of how their teaching and assessment methods affect pupils' approach to learning, and the qualities of that learning. Classroom practices, in reflecting this understanding, might then begin to incorporate this book's new perspective on the teaching of study skills.

The potential effects of this change in perspective in secondary education are wide-ranging. In encouraging pupils to take greater responsibility for their own learning, motivation and interest in learning could be enhanced. In fostering study skills at school, learning might be more effective and more readily applied to life in general. On the other hand, in failing to understand the teaching –learning process and to facilitate pupils' learning skill, schools and teachers could be accused of not educating pupils for their present needs, let alone those of the future.

Appendix 1

Studying at School Inventory

Please read these instructions carefully.

This questionnaire is designed to find out about how you study in your school work. There are no right or wrong answers. What is important is what you do or think.

Please read each sentence carefully and then show your response to it by drawing a circle round the appropriate letter.

A ($\sqrt{}\sqrt{}$) = always or almost always true
B ($\sqrt{}$) = generally true
C (?) = impossible to decide
D ($\times$) = not so often true
E ($\times\times$) = rarely or never true

Please start by filling in the details below:

SCHOOL ....

FORM YEAR ....

SEX Male/Female

DATE OF BIRTH . . . ./. . . ./. . . . AGE . . . . years

Do your subject choices, or your main interests, reflect:

A science bias (including Maths)　　　1
An arts bias (e.g. English, History)　　2
A language bias (e.g. French, Latin)　　3
None of these　　　　　　　　　　　4

(circle a code number 1–4 to answer the last question)

	√√	√	?	×	××
1　It is important to me that the teacher thinks that I have tried hard.	A	B	C	D	E
2　I try to memorise everything when I revise.	A	B	C	D	E
3　I don't have enough time to make notes of my own.	A	B	C	D	E
4　In written work I try to put over my own view whenever possible.	A	B	C	D	E
5　I rely on the teacher to tell me what to read.	A	B	C	D	E
6　It is important for me to get higher marks than other people.	A	B	C	D	E
7　My notes consist mostly of information or facts.	A	B	C	D	E
8　I organise what I am going to put in an answer before I write it.	A	B	C	D	E
9　I try to identify the underlying meaning in what I read.	A	B	C	D	E
10　I am fascinated by some of the work I do at school.	A	B	C	D	E
11　I like to be told precisely what to do in essays or other written work.	A	B	C	D	E
12　I don't have enough time to revise as much as I need.	A	B	C	D	E
13　When revising I try to summarise the material.	A	B	C	D	E

	√√	√	?	×	××
14 I try to use information from several books in my written work.	A	B	C	D	E
15 I enjoy competing with other pupils in school work.	A	B	C	D	E
16 I make notes only about the points I shall have to learn.	A	B	C	D	E
17 I don't feel that I organise my revision carefully enough.	A	B	C	D	E
18 I piece together notes from a variety of sources.	A	B	C	D	E
19 I worry when teachers criticise my work.	A	B	C	D	E
20 When reading I try to memorise everything.	A	B	C	D	E
21 In written exercises I write whatever I think of first.	A	B	C	D	E
22 I try to discuss with others a topic that I am trying to revise.	A	B	C	D	E
23 When school work is difficult I usually give up.	A	B	C	D	E
24 I try to revise everything as quickly as I possibly can.	A	B	C	D	E
25 When revising I like to be told precisely what to do.	A	B	C	D	E
26 I don't have enough time to make the notes I need.	A	B	C	D	E
27 When writing I consider how the various aspects link together.	A	B	C	D	E
28 I only revise what the teacher has told me to.	A	B	C	D	E

	√√	√	?	×	××

29 I get very worried if I get behind with
my work.   A   B   C   D   E

30 My written work consists mostly of
presenting information or facts.   A   B   C   D   E

31 I don't find enough time to revise in ways
which really satisfy me.   A   B   C   D   E

32 I try to include my own view whenever
possible, in making notes.   A   B   C   D   E

33 I generally leave my homework/prep.
until the last minute.   A   B   C   D   E

34 When I don't do well at school I feel
ashamed of myself.   A   B   C   D   E

35 When making notes I like to be told
precisely what to do.   A   B   C   D   E

36 I try to read everything as quickly as I
possibly can.   A   B   C   D   E

37 I try to summarise the material when
I make notes.   A   B   C   D   E

38 If I'm given something to do, I always
try to do it as well as possible.   A   B   C   D   E

39 I want teachers to know that they can
depend on me.   A   B   C   D   E

40 When I read I concentrate on the facts.   A   B   C   D   E

41 I don't feel that I organise my work
carefully enough.   A   B   C   D   E

42 When reading I try to work out the
connections between different aspects I
come across.   A   B   C   D   E

43 I'm expected to work out too many things
on my own.   A   B   C   D   E

	√√	√	?	×	××

44 It would make me feel bad if I disappointed the teacher.   A B C D E

45 I try to memorise my written work.   A B C D E

46 I don't find enough time to read in ways which really satisfy me.   A B C D E

47 When revising I consider how the various aspects link together.   A B C D E

48 If I do something badly, I try to work out why, so that I can do better next time.   A B C D E

49 There are a lot of lessons which I find exciting and challenging.   A B C D E

50 I like to be told precisely what to do in my reading.   A B C D E

51 I try to summarise the material in my written work.   A B C D E

52 I prefer to make my own notes when I can.   A B C D E

53 I feel really good when my friends can see that I've done well.   A B C D E

54 I concentrate on the facts when revising.   A B C D E

55 Often I ask myself questions about the things I hear in lessons or read in books.   A B C D E

56 It is important to me to do things better than other pupils, if I possibly can.   A B C D E

57 I try to make notes as quickly as I possibly can.   A B C D E

PLEASE MAKE SURE THAT YOU HAVE PUT A CIRCLE AGAINST *EVERY* QUESTION.

Instructions for scoring SASI

The transparent sheet 'Scoring SASI' consists of three columns that correspond to the three pages of questions in the SASI (*the original SASI consists of three pages of questions: page 1, 1–20; page 2, 21–40; page 3, 41–57*); the scale to which each question belongs and the numerical score for each response.

Place the left hand column of the transparent sheet directly over the responses to page 2 of SASI. Count up the scores for scale 1. Move to page 3 and the middle column and continue counting for scale 1. Move to page 4 and the right hand column and complete counting scale 1 score. Fill in total below. Repeat for scales 2 to 5.

Respondent	Scale 1	Scale 2	Scale 3	Scale 4	Scale 5
	/48	/48	/48	/48	/36

Scoring SASI

Q. 1–20 scale						Q. 21–40 scale						Q. 41–57 scale					
(4)	4	3	2	1	0	(3)	0	1	2	3	4	(3)	0	1	2	3	4
(2)	4	3	2	1	0	(1)	4	3	2	1	0	(1)	4	3	2	1	0
(3)	0	1	2	3	4	(5)	0	1	2	3	4	(5)	0	1	2	3	4
(1)	4	3	2	1	0	(3)	0	1	2	3	4	(4)	4	3	2	1	0
(5)	0	1	2	3	4	(2)	4	3	2	1	0	(2)	4	3	2	1	0
(4)	4	3	2	1	0	(3)	0	1	2	3	4	(3)	0	1	2	3	4
(2)	4	3	2	1	0	(1)	4	3	2	1	0	(1)	4	3	2	1	0
(3)	4	3	2	1	0	(5)	0	1	2	3	4	(5)	4	3	2	1	0
(1)	4	3	2	1	0	(4)	4	3	2	1	0	(4)	4	3	2	1	0
(4)	4	3	2	1	0	(2)	4	3	2	1	0	(2)	4	3	2	1	0
(2)	4	3	2	1	0	(3)	0	1	2	3	4	(1)	4	3	2	1	0
(3)	0	1	2	3	4	(1)	4	3	2	1	0	(5)	4	3	2	1	0
(1)	4	3	2	1	0	(5)	0	1	2	3	4	(4)	4	3	2	1	0
(5)	4	3	2	1	0	(4)	4	3	2	1	0	(2)	4	3	2	1	0
(4)	4	3	2	1	0	(2)	4	3	2	1	0	(1)	4	3	2	1	0
(2)	4	3	2	1	0	(3)	0	1	2	3	4	(4)	4	3	2	1	0
(3)	0	1	2	3	4	(1)	4	3	2	1	0	(3)	0	1	2	3	4
(1)	4	3	2	1	0	(5)	4	3	2	1	0						
(4)	4	3	2	1	0	(4)	4	3	2	1	0						
(2)	4	3	2	1	0	(2)	4	3	2	1	0						

Appendix 2

Some Learning to Learn Materials

Passage A
African self-help urged

The US Secretary of State, Mr George Shultz, told African countries yesterday to carry out their promises for thrusting economic reforms and to expand the opportunities for individual initiative if they expect to promote successful development.

Speaking on the second day of the UN General Assembly's special session on Africa's economic crisis, Mr Shultz offered American support 'in the search for worthwhile approaches to long-term development'.

But he disappointed the Africans by failing to address the question of how much financial aid the US would provide. 'The United States, with its own budgetary concerns, cannot meet all the African requests for assistance. So we are exploring creative alternatives, mostly through multinational institutions,' he said.

While Mr Shultz tried to show support for African efforts and self-help, his speech emphasised the wide gap between American and African economic views.

Britain and France have also avoided any direct offer of assistance. Sir Geoffrey Howe suggested that Africa might do more to help itself. 'Africa has the capacity to feed itself. Yet hunger persists in many places . . . management efficiency must be improved, public spending brought under control and subsidies adjusted . . . (there must be) a climate favourable to private investment, freed of the restrictions of the past.'

Sir Geoffrey praised the Africans for the seriousness of their approach to their development goals.

Mr Shultz spoke of the priority needs to stimulate the private sector and encourage free private enterprise and individual initiative. 'We have seen how now discredited orthodoxies about state-directed development gave rise to misguided policies that stifle individual initiative by policies that in practice have given inadequate incentives to African farmers and created a long-term decline in food production.'

At one stage he departed from the prepared text of his address to denounce apartheid as 'unacceptable to its own right'.

Most African countries, which lean towards various forms of socialism, believe that governments must play the central economic role.

So, the Africans regard the current General Assembly session mainly as an opportunity for developed nations to offer more aid for African development. Africa is asking for $80 billion over the next four years in grants and in debt release.

So far only two Western countries have responded positively. The Netherlands has said it would cancel payments of interest and principal on its aid to poor African countries for five years, which will amount to $80 million in debt release. Canada promised sub-Saharan countries a 15-year moratorium on both repayments for a total of $25 million in debt release.

The Soviet Union in its speech took the opposite approach. The Soviet delegate supported Africa's 'just demands' against the West to compensate for 'neo-colonialist plunder'.

This article by Jane Rosen first appeared in The Guardian, *29 May, 1986.*

Passage B
Housing in Brazilian Favelas

There are two types of favela. In one type live the migrants who have lived in Sao Paulo for a number of years and have gradually improved their home so that it has a bit more than basic amenities. These homes have electricity, showers, toilets and maybe even a TV. The homes are built of concrete and so are resistant to wind and rain. However the families who live in these places are still poor, it is just that they have managed to save up money in the length of time that they have stayed in Sao Paulo.

In the second type are the newly arrived migrants who have very little money, and these people live elsewhere. They construct a wooden shack on the first piece of ground they find (it doesn't belong to them) and then more wooden shacks are built around this one. This is how a favela starts and then keeps on growing. Without a sewage system or water supply the sanitary conditions deteriorate rapidly.

There are four million people (one-third of Sao Paulo's total population) who live in favelas. The favelas are found on the outskirts of the town, some as far as 25 kilometres from the city centre.

Passage C
Improving Shanty Towns

The way to stop shanty towns growing up is either to give migrants money to rent cheap accommodation or to give the migrant the accommodation. Either way the government spends an enormous amount of money. In the city that I designed there are blocks of high-rise flats to accommodate migrants. These flats are very close to the industrial areas and will encourage the migrants to find a job. There are plenty of these apartment blocks. Some migrants may be very tempted to set up shacks on some of the green areas, maybe even on the football pitch! To avoid this the city will have to provide ample accommodation for the migrants inside the city. If there are not enough places for people to live and they are forcibly removed from the green areas, then shanty towns will be set up around the city (like in Sao Paulo, up to 25 kilometres away from the centre). My city has enough accommodation.

The simple answer to providing adequate services (electricity, sewerage, water) to all housing is to install it when the housing is being built. This means that pipes will have to be laid under the streets and a sewage works will have to be in the area. Electricity can be generated from the water in the lake. If the population continues to expand, more electricity plants will have to be made to cope with the increased demand. The water must be pure and in ample supply. This means having a water supply close at hand as well as purification plants – which my city has. Garbage collections must be frequent and efficient in a large city. To do this work some of the migrants could be employed doing jobs like garbage collection and street cleaning as well as other basic, but necessary, jobs.

Passage D
Is Development in the Third World
Always a Slow Process?

The lack of development is due to several factors. Firstly there is the lack of understanding and unwillingness to accept modern machinery. Many farmers do not know how to repair or use modern machinery and so revert to their traditional ways, leaving tractors to rust in the fields. There is a lack of modernisation in the areas of irrigation and crop storage. It is often the lack of money which deters the farmer from having a steel storage bin or a sprinkler system. Fertilisers and insecticides are not used in large enough quantities (because of a lack of money) to have a tremendous effect on crop output and so not enough surplus is made by governments to subsidise farmers. Couple this with the fact that the governments of many less developed countries are dictators who spend a large amount of money on unnecessary arms and munitions and you really do have a big problem in persuading governments to spend enough money on helping the poor and developing farming techniques.

The slow process is, therefore, due to the lack of money available to buy in modernisation to keep up with improvements in methods of farming. It is a vicious cycle because the less the farmers make the less they can spend on improving and in this way the development is very slow. It can only be speeded up if they are helped by the developed countries.

References

1 M. Marland (1981) 'Information Skills in the Secondary Curriculum', *Schools Council Curriculum Bulletin*, 9. London: Methuen Educational Ltd.

2 R. Tabberer and J. Allman (1983) *Introducing Study Skills: An Appraisal of Initiatives at 16+*. Windsor: NFER/Nelson.

3 C. Swatridge (1982) 'The Aptitude for and Attitudes Towards Independent Study of Students on Advanced Level GCE Courses', unpublished PhD thesis, University of Nottingham.

4 R. R. Thompson (1982) 'Educational Aims and Pedagogical Principles among Sixth-Formers and their Teachers', unpublished MA extended essay, University of Leeds.

5 J. Dean (1978) '16–19 Study Problems', *NFER Research in Progress No. 2*. Slough: NFER.

6 I. P. Selmes (1985) 'Approaches to Learning at Secondary School: their Identification and Facilitation', unpublished PhD thesis, University of Edinburgh.

7 M. M. Roberts (1981) 'Establishing a study skills course for sixth-form students', *Educational Research*, 24, pp. 24–30.

8 Department of Education and Science (1986) *English School Leavers 1983–84*, Statistical Bulletin.

9 Scottish Education Department (1986) *School Leavers' Qualifications*, Statistical Bulletin.

10 N. J. Entwistle and B. Kozeki (1985) 'Relationships between school motivation, approaches to studying and attainment, among British and Hungarian adolescents', *British Journal of Educational Psychology*, 55, pp. 124–37.

11 E. Spencer (1983) *Writing Matters Across the Curriculum*. Edinburgh: Scottish Council for Research in Education.

12 J. Nisbet and J. Shucksmith (1986) *Learning Strategies*. London: Routledge and Kegan Paul.

13 J. Ruddock, D. Hopkins, S. Groundwater-Smith and B. Labbett (1984) 'Independent study: books and libraries in the academic sixth-form', *Journal of Curriculum Studies*, 16, pp. 198–200.

14 N. Reid (1975) 'Developing Study Skills in the Reading Process'. Paper read at the Sixth New Zealand International Reading Association Conference, Hamilton, New Zealand.

15 H. T. Morse and G. H. McClure (1964) *Selected Items for the Testing of Study Skills and Critical Thinking*, Bulletin 15. Washington: NCSS.

16 T. Buzan (1974) *Use Your Head*. London: BBC Publications.

17 D. Rowntree (1970) *Learn How to Study*. London: Macdonald.

18 F. T. Scapaticci (1977) 'A Study of SQ3R and Select and Recite Reading and Study Skills Methods in College Classes', doctoral dissertation, Leigh University.

19 A. D. Burgen (1982) *How to Study: A Practical Guide*. London: Harrap.

20 R. Tabberer and J. Allman (1980) *Study Skills*, Newsletter No. 1. Slough: NFER.

21 D. B. Jackson (1973) *The Exam Secret*. Tadworth, Surrey: Elliot Right Way Books.
22 H. Maddox (1963) *How to Study*. London: Pan.
23 S. Harri-Augstein and L. F. Thomas (1979) 'Learning conversations: a person centred approach to a self-organised learning', *British Journal of Guidance and Counselling*, 7, pp. 80–92.
24 N. J. Entwistle, J. Thompson and J. J. Wilson (1974) 'Motivation and study habits', *Higher Education*, 3, pp. 379–8.
25 S. Harri-Augstein, M. Smith and L. Thomas (1982) *Reading to Learn*. London: Methuen Educational Ltd.
26 A. Main (1980) *Encouraging Effective Learning*. Edinburgh: Scottish Academic Press.
27 G. Gibbs (1981) *Teaching Students to Learn – A Student Centred Approach*. Milton Keynes: Open University Press.
28 D. H. Hamblin (1981) *Teaching Study Skills*. Oxford: Basil Blackwell.
29 A. Irving (1982) *Starting to Teach Study Skills*. London: Edward Arnold.
30 I. P. Selmes (1986) 'Approaches to normal learning tasks adopted by senior secondary school pupils', *British Educational Research Journal*, 12.1, pp. 15–28.
31 F. Marton, D. J. Hounsell and N. J. Entwistle (1984) *The Experience of Learning*. Edinburgh: Scottish Academic Press.
32 P. Ramsden, J. A. Bowden and D. G. Beswick (1986) 'Learning processes and learning skills' in J. T. E. Richardson, M. W. Eysenck and D. Warren-Piper (eds) *Student Learning: Research in Education and Cognitive Psychology*. Windsor: SRHE/NFER-Nelson.
33 J. Nisbet and J. Shucksmith (1984) 'The seventh sense', *Scottish Educational Review*, 16, pp. 75–87.

Bibliography

Burgen, A. D. (1982) *How to Study: A Practical Guide*. London: Harrap.

Buzan, T. (1974) *Use Your Head*. London: BBC Publications.

Dean, J. (1978) '16–19 Study Problems', *NFER Research in Progress*, No. 2. Slough: NFER.

Department of Education and Science (1986) *English School Leavers 1983–84*, Statistical Bulletin.

Entwistle, N. J. and Kozeki, B. (1985) 'Relationships between school motivation, approaches to studying and attainment, among British and Hungarian adolescents', *British Journal of Educational Psychology*, 55, pp. 124–37.

Entwistle, N. J., Thompson, J. and Wilson, J. J. (1974) 'Motivation and study habits', *Higher Education*, 3, pp. 379–98.

Gibbs, G. (1981) *Teaching Students to Learn – A Student Centred Approach*. Milton Keynes: Open University Press.

Hamblin, D. H. (1981) *Teaching Study Skills*. Oxford: Basil Blackwell.

Harri-Augstein, S., Smith, M. and Thomas, L. (1982) *Reading to Learn*. London: Methuen Educational Ltd.

Harri-Augstein, S. and Thomas, L. (1979) 'Learning conversations: a person centred approach to a self-organised learning', *British Journal of Guidance and Counselling*, 7, pp. 80–92.

Irving, A. (ed.) (1982) *Starting to Teach Study Skills*. London: Edward Arnold.

Jackson, D. B. (1973) *The Exam Secret*. Tadworth, Surrey: Elliot Right Way Books.

Maddox, H. (1963) *How To Study*. London: Pan.

Main, A. (1980) *Encouraging Effective Learning*. Edinburgh: Scottish Academic Press.

Marland, M. (1981) 'Information Skills in the Secondary Curriculum', *Schools Council Curriculum Bulletin* 9. London: Methuen Educational Ltd.

Marton, F., Hounsell, D. J. and Entwistle, N. J. (1984) *The Experience of Learning*. Edinburgh: Scottish Academic Press.

Morse, H. T. and McClure, G. H. (1964) *Selected Items for the Testing of Study Skills and Critical Thinking*, Bulletin 15. Washington: NCSS.

Nisbet, J. and Shucksmith, J. (1984) 'The seventh sense', *Scottish Educational Review*, 16, pp. 75–87.

Nisbet, J. and Shucksmith, J. (1986) *Learning Strategies*. London: Routledge and Kegan Paul.

Ramsden, P., Bowden, J. A., and Beswick, D. G. (1986) 'Learning processes and learning skills' in Richardson, J. T. E., Eysenck, M. W., and Warren-Piper, D. (eds.) *Student Learning: Research in Education and Cognitive Psychology*. Windsor: SRHE/NFER – Nelson.

Reid, N. (1975) 'Developing Study Skills in the Reading Process'. Paper read at the

Sixth New Zealand International Reading Association Conference, Hamilton, New Zealand.

Roberts, M. M. (1981) 'Establishing a study skills course for sixth-form students', *Educational Research*, 24, pp. 24–30.

Rowntree, D. (1970) *Learn How to Study*. London: Macdonald.

Ruddock, J., Hopkins, D., Groundwater-Smith, S. and Labbett, B. (1984) 'Independent study: books and libraries in the academic sixth-form, *Journal of Curriculum Studies*, 16, pp. 198–200.

Scapaticci, F. T. (1977) 'A study of SQ3R and Select and Recite Reading and Study Skills Methods in College Classes', doctoral dissertation, Leigh University.

SED (1986) *School Leavers' Qualifications*, Statistical Bulletin.

SED and SEB (1982) *Full-time Education after S4: A Statistical Study*. Dalkeith: Scottish Education Department and Scottish Examination Board.

Selmes, I. P. (1985) 'Approaches to Learning at Secondary School: their Identification and Facilitation', unpublished PhD thesis, University of Edinburgh.

Selmes, I. P. (1986) 'Approaches to normal learning tasks adopted by senior secondary school pupils', *British Educational Research Journal*, 12, 1.

Spencer, E. (1983a) *Writing Matters Across the Curriculum*. Edinburgh: (Scottish Council for Research in Education.

Spencer, E. (1983b) *Written Work in Scottish Secondary Schools*. Edinburgh: Scottish Council for Research in Education.

Swatridge, C. (1982) 'The Aptitude for and Attitudes Towards Independent Study of Students on Advanced Level GCE Courses', unpublished PhD thesis, University of Nottingham.

Tabberer, R. and Allman, J. (1980) *Study Skills*, Newsletter No. 1. Slough: NFER.

Tabberer, R. and Allman, J. (1983) *Introducing Study Skills: An Appraisal of Initiatives at 16+*. Windsor: NFER/Nelson.

Thompson, R. R. (1982) 'Educational Aims and Pedagogical Principles among Sixth-Formers and their Teachers', unpublished MA extended essay, University of Leeds.

Index